Principle in A

Coventry Patmore

Alpha Editions

This edition published in 2024

ISBN 9789362514202

Design and Setting By
Alpha Editions
www.alphaedis.com
Email - info@alphaedis.com

As per information held with us this book is in Public Domain.
This book is a reproduction of an important historical work.
Alpha Editions uses the best technology to reproduce historical work
in the same manner it was first published to preserve its original nature.
Any marks or number seen are left intentionally to preserve.

Contents

PREFACE	- 1 -
I PRINCIPLE IN ART	- 2 -
II REAL APPREHENSION	- 5 -
III SEERS, THINKERS, AND TALKERS	- 9 -
I	- 9 -
II	- 11 -
IV POSSIBILITIES AND PERFORMANCES	- 14 -
V CHEERFULNESS IN LIFE AND ART	- 17 -
VI THE POINT OF REST IN ART	- 20 -
VII IMAGINATION	- 23 -
VIII PATHOS	- 26 -
IX POETICAL INTEGRITY	- 29 -
X THE POETRY OF NEGATION	- 32 -
XI THE LIMITATIONS OF GENIUS	- 35 -
XII LOVE AND POETRY	- 37 -
XIII KEATS	- 41 -
XIV WHAT SHELLEY WAS	- 44 -
XV BLAKE	- 49 -
XVI ROSSETTI AS A POET	- 52 -
XVII MR. SWINBURNE'S SELECTIONS	- 56 -
XVIII ARTHUR HUGH CLOUGH	- 59 -
XIX EMERSON	- 62 -
XX CRABBE AND SHELLEY	- 66 -
XXI SHALL SMITH HAVE A STATUE?	- 69 -

XXII IDEAL AND MATERIAL GREATNESS IN ARCHITECTURE	- 71 -
XXIII "OLD ENGLISH" ARCHITECTURE, ANCIENT AND MODERN	- 75 -
XXIV ARCHITECTURAL STYLES	- 78 -
I	- 78 -
II	- 81 -
III	- 85 -
IV	- 88 -
V	- 91 -
XXV THOUGHTS ON KNOWLEDGE, OPINION, AND INEQUALITY	- 97 -

PREFACE

WITH one exception, namely the last Paper in the Collection, which appeared in the *Fortnightly Review*, all these Essays were printed in the *St. James's Gazette* during the editorship of Mr. Greenwood. The Essay on "Architectural Styles" contains a summary of principles which I stated, some thirty years ago, in various Articles, chiefly in the *Edinburgh Review*. As this Essay now stands, I hope that readers, who have knowledge enough to enable them to judge, will find in it an example of the kind of criticism which I have advocated earlier in the volume.

COVENTRY PATMORE.

I

PRINCIPLE IN ART

It is not true, though it has so often been asserted, that criticism is of no use or of little use to art. This notion prevails so widely only because—among us at least—criticism has not been criticism. To criticise is to judge; to judge requires judicial qualification; and this is quite a different thing from a natural sensitiveness to beauty, however much that sensitiveness may have become heightened by converse with refined and beautiful objects of nature and works of art. "Criticism," which has been the outcome only of such sensitiveness and such converse, may be, and often is,—delightful reading, and is naturally far more popular than criticism which is truly judicial. The pseudo-criticism, of which we have had such floods during the past half-century, delights by sympathy with, and perhaps expansion of, our own sensations; true criticism appeals to the intellect, and rebukes the reader as often as it does the artist for his ignorance and his mistakes. Such criticism may not be able to produce good art; but bad art collapses at the contact of its breath, as the steam in the cylinder of an engine collapses on each admission of the spray of cold water; and thus, although good criticism cannot produce art, it removes endless hindrances to its production, and tends to provide art with its chief motive-power, a public prepared to acknowledge it. The enunciation of a single principle has sometimes, almost at a blow, revolutionised not only the technical practice of an art, but the popular taste with regard to it. Strawberry Hill Gothic vanished like a nightmare when Pugin for the first time authoritatively asserted and proved that architectural decoration could never properly be an addition to constructive features, but only a fashioning of them. The truth was manifest at once to amateur as well as to architect; and this one principle proves to have contained a power even of popular culture far greater than all the splendid "sympathetic" criticism which followed during the next fifty years. And it has done nothing but good, whereas the latter kind of writing, together with much good, has done much harm. Pugin's insight did not enable him to discover the almost equally clear and simple principle which governs the special form of decoration that properly characterises each of the great styles of architecture. Therefore, while his law of constructional decoration compelled all succeeding "critics" to keep within its bounds, they were still free to give the rein to mere fancy as to the nature of the decoration itself; and this has been becoming worse and worse in proportion as critics and architects of genius, but of no principle, have departed from the dry tradition of decorative form which prevailed in Pugin's day, and which finds its orthodox expression in Parker's *Glossary* and the elementary works of Bloxam and Rickman. Sensitiveness or natural "taste," apart from principle, is, in art, what love is apart from truth in morals. The stronger it is, the further it is likely to go wrong. Nothing can be more tenderly "felt" than a school of painting which is now much in favour; but, for want of knowledge and masculine principle, it has come to delight in representing ugliness and corruption in place of health and beauty. Venus or Hebe becomes, in its hands, nothing but a *Dame aux Camélias* in the last stage of moral and physical deterioration. A few infallible and, when once uttered, self-evident principles would at once put a stop to this sort of representation amongartists; and the public would soon learn to be repelled by what now most attracts them, being thenceforward guided by a critical conscience, which is the condition of "*good* taste."

There is little that is conclusive or fruitful in any of the criticism of the present day. The very name that it has chosen, "Æsthetics," contains an implied admission of its lack of virility or principle. We do not think of Lessing's *Laocoön*, which is one of the finest pieces of critical writing in the world, as belonging to "Æsthetics"; and, like it, the critical sayings of Goethe and Coleridge seem to appertain to a science deserving a nobler name—a science in which truth stands first and feeling second, and of which the conclusions are demonstrable and irreversible. A critic of the present day, in attempting to describe the difference between the usual construction of a passage by Fletcher and one by Shakespeare, would beat helplessly about the bush, telling us many things about the different sorts of feelings awakened by the one and by the other, and concluding, and desiring to conclude, nothing. Coleridge in a single sentence defines the difference, and establishes Shakespeare's immeasurable superiority with the clearness and finality of a mathematical statement; and the delight of the reader of Shakespeare is for ever heightened because it is less than before a zeal without knowledge.

There already exists, in the writings and sayings of Aristotle, Hegel, Lessing, Goethe, and others, the greater part of the materials necessary for the formation of a body of Institutes of Art which would supersede and extinguish nearly all the desultory chatter which now passes for criticism, and which would go far to form a true and abiding popular taste—one which could render some reason for its likings and dislikings. The man, however, who could put such materials together and add such as are wanting does not live; or at any rate he is not known. Hegel might have done it, had his artistic perception been as fine and strong as his intellect; which would then have expressed its conclusions without the mist of obscurity in which, for nearly all readers, they are at present shrouded. In the meantime it would be well if the professed critic would remember that criticism is not the expression, however picturesque and glowing, of the faith that is in him, but the rendering of sound and intelligible reasons for that faith.

II

REAL APPREHENSION

"MAN," says Dr. Newman, "is not a reasoning animal; he is a seeing, feeling, contemplating, acting animal." To see rightly is the first of human qualities; right feeling and right acting are usually its consequences. There are two ways of seeing: one is to comprehend, which is to see all round a thing, or to embrace it; one is to apprehend, which is to see it in part, or to take hold of it. A thing may be really taken hold of which is much too big for embracing. Real apprehension implies reality in that which is apprehended. You cannot "take hold" of that which is nothing. The notional grasp which some people seem to have of clouds and mares' nests is a totally different thing from real apprehension; though what this difference is could scarcely be made clear to those who have no experience of the latter. A man may not be able to convey to another his real apprehension of a thing; but there will be something in his general character and way of discoursing which will convince you, if you too are a man acquainted with realities, that he has truly got hold of what he professes to have got hold of, and you will be wary of denying what he affirms. The man of real apprehensions, or the truly sensible man, has no opinions. Many things may be dubious to him; but if he is compelled to act without knowledge, he does so promptly, being prompt to discern which of the doubtful ways before him is the least questionable, on the ground of such evidence as he has. As to what he sees to be true or right, he does not argue with the person who differs from him upon a vital point, but only avoids his company, or, if he be of an irascible temperament, feels inclined to knock him down. Of course there are some people who see things which do not exist; but this is lunacy, and beyond the scope of these remarks. Real apprehension is emphatically the quality which constitutes "good sense." Common good sense has a real apprehension of innumerable things which those who add to good sense learning and reflection may comprehend; but there is much that must for ever remain matter only of real apprehension to the best seers; that is to say, everything in which the infinite has a part, *i.e.* all religion, all virtue as distinguished from temporary expediency, the grounds of all true art, etc. A man may have an immense acquaintance with facts; he may have all history and the whole circle of the sciences on the tip of his tongue; he may be the author of a classical system of logic, or may have so cunningly elaborated a false theory of nature as to puzzle and infuriate the wisest of men: and yet may not really apprehend any part of the truth of life which is properly human knowledge. At the present time it is by politics chiefly that the difference between the two great classes of men is made apparent. For the first time in English history, party limitations coincide almost exactly with the limitations which separate silly from sensible men. If you talk with a sincere Gladstonian—and, wonderful to say, there are still many such—you will soon find that he has no real apprehension of anything. He only feebly and foolishly opines.

It is not to be concluded from what has been said that the possession of the apprehending faculty in any way supersedes the good of learning. The power of really apprehending is nothing in the absence of realities to be apprehended. In the great field of ordinary social relationships and duties the subject-matter of such apprehension is largely supplied by individual experience, and the exercise by most men of that faculty is in the main limited to these; so that the praise of "goodsense" has acquired a much narrower signification than it ought to bear. Genius is nothing but great good sense, or real apprehension, exercised upon objects more or less out of common sight; and the chief ingredient of even the highest and most heroic sanctity is the same apprehension taking hold upon spiritual truths and applying them to the conduct of the interior as well as the exterior life. Men with great strength of real apprehension are easily capable of things which inferior characters regard as great self-sacrifices; though to them such things are no more sacrifice than in an ordinary man it would be to exchange a ton of lead for a pound of gold. "Their hearts do not forget the things their eyes have seen;" and persons like General Gordon or Sir Thomas More would stare if you called anything they did or suffered by the name of sacrifice.

You cannot read the writings of Newman, Hooker, Pascal, and St. Augustine, without being strongly impressed with the presumption that they have a real apprehension of the things they profess to believe; and, since they do not justify in any other way the theory that they are lunatics, a right-minded reader is likewise disposed to think that what they have thus seen exists, and that his not having seen such things does not materially diminish that probability.

And here it may be well to recur to the text of these remarks: "Man is not a reasoning animal; he is a seeing, feeling, contemplating, acting animal." All men properly so called—but a good many who walk upright on two legs cannot properly be so called—are seeing, feeling, and acting animals; but very few men, indeed, have as yet attained to be contemplating animals, though the act of contemplation exercised upon the highest objects is, according to all great philosophers, even pagan, the act for which he is created and in which his final perfection and felicity are attained. The act of real apprehension, as it is exerted by ordinary men, and even for the most part by men of extraordinary vigour of intellectual vision, is momentary, however permanent may be its effect upon their principles and lives. Men of vigorous apprehension look at the heavens of truth, as it were, through a powerful telescope, and see instantly as realities many living lights which are quite invisible to the common eye. But contemplation—a faculty rare in all times, but wellnigh unheard of in ours—is like the photographic plate which finds stars that no telescope can discover, by simply setting its passively expectant gaze in certain indicated directions so long and steadily that telescopically invisible bodies become apparent by accumulation of impression. Such men are prophets andapostles, whether canonical or not. It is by the instrumentality of such men that religions are established and upheld; and the term "verifiable religion" is a piece of mere nineteenth-century slang, when applied to the examination of dogma by such as have probably never had the remotest apprehension of any spiritual reality. Certain facts of history relating to religion may or may not be capable of "verification" to the multitude; but the dogmas which are the substance of a religion, can only be really apprehended—assuming them to be real and apprehensible—by the exceedingly few to whom the highest powers of contemplation, which are usually the accompaniments of equally extraordinary virtues, are accorded. The mass of mankind must receive and hold these things as they daily receive and hold a thousand other things—laws, customs, traditions, the grounds of common moralities, etc.—by faith; their real apprehension in such matters extending for the most part only to the discernment of the reasonableness of so receiving and holding them.

Now this faculty and habit of really apprehending things, even in its lower and not uncommon degree, is an immeasurable advantage; but it has its drawback. Those who possess it are singularly capable of committing the unpardonable sin, the sin against knowledge. "Father, forgive them,for they know not what they do" is a petition which He who spoke these words could not have offered for deeds or denials in clear opposition to what a man knows to be true and good. "My name is in him and He will not pardon." All men agree in calling the spirit of truth—which is the spirit by which truth is really apprehended—holy; and to deny this spirit in deliberate action may, without any appeal to Christian doctrine, be proved to be unpardonable by the way such action is known to influence a man's character. A single act of such denial, if it be in some great and vital matter, often seems to destroy the soul. History affords more than one example of a statesman who has begun life with an eagle eye for truth, a strong and tender love of honour, and everything that makes a man among men. At some crisis of temptation he chooses personal ambition before some clearly apprehended duty of patriotism; and his whole nature seems thenceforward changed: he drops like a scorched fly from the flame—

Then takes his doom, to limp and crawl,
Blind and despised, from fall to fall.

But the least practical denial of real apprehension of the truth is, to such as have ever had a conscience and have observed themselves, demonstrably unpardonable, inasmuch as it destroys a portion of the capacity of the soul. "The remnant" may, indeed, "become a great nation," but it will be still and for ever a remnant of what it would have been, had it preserved the integrity of its fidelity.

If we knew the secrets of the lives of those—alas! innumerable—who seem to have no real apprehension of anything, none of the light which it is said lighteth every man that cometh into the world, it would probably be found that they have not been born without, but have forfeited their noblest human heritage, by repeated practical denials of the things which they have seen.

III

SEERS, THINKERS, AND TALKERS

I

THE intellect, the understanding or discursive reason, and the memory, it need scarcely be said, are three distinct faculties; yet in their exercise and the character they acquire for their possessors, they are apt to be confused, and that not without damage to the public and private interests of those who make the mistake. Intellect, though it is constantly spoken of as synonymous with understanding, is really an incomparably rarer quality, the difference being that which subsists between "genius" and "talent"; and to ignorant persons a ready and well-stored memory, which is consistent with the almost total defect of either of the nobler faculties, is often regarded as a combination of both.

The intellect is the faculty of the "seer." It discerns truth as a living thing; and, according as it is in less or greater power, it discerns with amore or less far-seeing glance the relationships of principles to each other, and of facts, circumstances, and the realities of nature to principles, without anything that can be properly called ratiocination. It cannot be cultivated, as the understanding and memory can be and need to be; and it cannot in the ordinary course of things be injured, except by one means—namely, dishonesty, that is, habitual denial by the will, for the sake of interested or vicious motives, of its own perceptions. Genius and high moral—not necessarily physical—courage are therefore found to be constant companions. Indeed, it is difficult to say how far an absolute moral courage in acknowledging intuitions may not be of the very nature of genius: and whether it might not be described as a sort of interior sanctity which dares to see and confess to itself that it sees, though its vision should place it in a minority of one. Everybody feels that genius is, in a sort, infallible. That it is so, is indeed an "identical proposition." So far as a man is not infallible in what he professes to see, he is not a man of genius—that is, he is not a seer. It is by no figure of speech that genius is called inspiration. Dr. Newman somewhere observes that St. Augustine and some of the primitive teachers of the Church wandered at will through all the mazes of theology with an intuitive orthodoxy of genius.

Although this faculty of direct vision is very rare in comparison with those of ordinary ratiocination and memory, it is not nearly so rare as is supposed by such as measure genius by its manifestations in philosophy, science, art, or statesmanship. For one seer who has the accomplishments and opportunities whereby his faculty can be turned to public account, there are scores and hundreds who possess and exercise for their private use their extraordinary perceptive powers. To whom has it not happened, at one time or other, to witness the instantaneous shattering of some splendid edifice of reasoning and memory by the brief Socratic interrogation of some ignoramus who could see?

No mortal intellect or genius is other than very partial, and, even in that partial character, imperfect. Absolute genius would be nothing more nor less than the sight of all things at once in their relationship and origin; but the most imperfect genius has an infinite value—not only because it is actual sight of truth, but also and still more because it is a peculiar mode of seeing, a reflection of truth coloured but not obscured by the individual character, which in each man of genius is entirely unique. This unique character is, in its expression, what is called "style"—the sure mark of genius, though the world at large is unable to distinguish "style" from manner, or even from mannerism. Incomparably the highest and fortunately the least uncommon form of genius is wisdom in the conduct of life; for this form involves in a far greater degree than any other the constant exercise of that courage which is inseparable from genius. The saint is simply a person who has so strong and clear a sight of the truth which concerns him individually, and such courage to confess his vision, that he is always ready to become a "confessor" under any extremity of persecution.

True statesmanship is another form of wisdom in the conduct of life; and this is perhaps the rarest of all forms in which genius manifests itself, because it requires a combination of inferior faculties and opportunities which is almost as rare as genius. Poetry is the only near rival of true statesmanship in this respect. The immensely wider and more various range of vision which the great poet exercises when compared with other artists, together with the necessity for the combined working of many lesser faculties and laboriously acquired accomplishments, has always made of the poet the ideal "genius" in the world's esteem. The separate insights into the significance of form, colour, and sound, upon which the arts of the sculptor, painter, and musician are founded, must be included in the vision of the poet of the first rank.

What is called "common sense" is much more nearly allied to genius, or true intellect, than either talent, which is the outcome of the discursive reason, or learning, which is that of memory. Compared with the sunlight by which the purer intellect sees, common sense is the light of a foggy day, which is good enough to see near objects and to avoid mischief by. Science is generally considered to be the outcome solely of the observation of facts and the discursive reason; but in men like Kepler, Newton, and Faraday there is no lack of "the vision and the faculty divine." The discovery of gravitation by the fall of an apple was pure vision; and it is doubtful whether there was ever a Smith's Prizeman who had not a touch of a higher faculty than that which gropes step by step from premises to conclusions.

A ghastly semblance of genius is often retained by such persons as once had it, but have ruined it by denying it in action, and by endeavouring to prostitute it to selfish or vicious interests. Their judicial blindness is the reverse of that which was inflicted upon Tiresias for daring to gaze upon unveiled wisdom. He could no longer see the world; they can no longer see the heavens. But their original genius takes the perverted form of an intuitive craft in pursuing their ends which is noless amazing, and which, in statesmen especially, is commonly mistaken by the people for the holy faculty which has been quenched.

To be a man of talent a man must be able to think; to be a man of genius he must be able not to think, and especially to abstain from the crazy wool-gathering which is ordinarily regarded as thought. "The harvest of a quiet eye," and the learning of the ear which listens in a silence even of thought, are the wealth of the pure intellect. And the fainter and the more remote the whispers which are heard in such silence, the more precious and potential are they likely to be. It is no condemnation of the thought of Hegel that he is reported to have replied to some question as to the meaning of a passage in his writings, that "he knew what it meant when he wrote it." This thought, too subtle or too simple for expression and memory, might, if held down and compelled to manifest itself more explicitly, have moved mankind.

Genius is a great disturber. It is always a new thing, and demands of old things that they should make a place for it, which cannot be done without more or less inconvenient rearrangements; and as it seems to threaten even worse trouble than it is finally found to give, it is generally hated and resisted on its first appearance. Moreover, to the eye which is not congenial the fresh manifestation of genius in almost any kind has something in it alarming and revolting; and it is welcomed with an "Ugh, ugh! the horrid thing! It's alive!" A man of genius who is also a man of sense will never complain of such a reception from his fellows. Their opposition is even respectable from their point of view and with their faculties of beholding.

II

Genius, like sanctity, is commonly more or less foolish in the eyes of the world. Its riches are "the riches of secret places"; and they so much exceed, in its esteem, those that are considered riches by the common sense of men, that its neglect of the ordinary goods of life often amounts to real imprudence—imprudence even from its own point of view, whereby it is bound to avoid hindrances to its free life and exercise. The follies, however, of a Blake or a Hartley Coleridge are venial when compared with those of the thoughtful and prudent fool—the fool in respect of great things, as the other is in respect of small. Who can measure the harm that may be done to the world by a thoughtful and earnest fool—one who starts from data which he is too dull to verify, and who multiplies his mistakes in proportion tothe perspicuity and extent of his deductions? The man of "talent" who is merely such, is not a very common phenomenon—for "talent" is in great part the product of culture; which "genius," or the power of seeing, is not. Most persons of talent still possess a share of that obscure kind of genius called common sense, which keeps them from taking up with false principles and following them into wild conclusions. We need, however, only recall some famous figures in the present and past generation in order to be assured that immense talent is consistent with an almost complete deficiency of real insight. When the discursive understanding is in great force, and has at its command abundant stores of external information, we behold a power that may work the ruin of empires amid applauding peoples, though it can never build them up. The natural and exact sciences are the proper fields for the exertions of such a faculty.

Stupid persons fancy they derogate from the supremacy of the pure intellect or genius by observing that it is always associated with a vivid imagination, which they regard as a faculty for seeing things as they are not. Shelley made a mistake in a totally different direction when he declared that the imagination is the power by which spiritual things are discerned; whereas thetruth is that intellect is the power by which such things are discerned, and imagination is that by which they are expressed. Sensible things alone can be expressed fully and directly by sensible terms. Symbols and parables, and metaphors—which are parables on a small scale—are the only means of adequately conveying, or rather hinting, supersensual knowledge. "He spake not without a parable." Hebrew, Greek, Indian, and Egyptian religions all spoke in parables; and poets deal in images and parables simply because there is no other vehicle for what they have to say. "The things which are unseen may be known by the things which are seen," but only by way of symbol and parable. Imagination, though it is not, as Shelley says it is, the power of spiritual insight, is its invariable concomitant; and even that dull kinsman of genius, common sense, would feel sadly hampered in its endeavours to convey its perceptions to the minds of others, were it wholly without the faculty of speaking in parables.

It has often been noted that men of genius have bad memories, and that persons having extraordinary memories, like Cardinal Mezzofanti, have little else. The truth is that there are two quite distinct kinds of memory: the memory for external facts and words, apart from their significance; and the memory for spiritual facts and principles. Theman of genius, who may have no special reason for cultivating the lower kind of memory, may even find it rather a hindrance than a help. His prayer is, "Let not my heart forget the things mine eyes have seen." So long as his heart retains the significance of the facts he has seen and the words he has heard, he is willing to let the words and the facts go, as a man casts away the shells after he has eaten the oysters. The "well-informed" person commonly differs from the man of genius in this: that he carries about with him all the shells of all the oysters he has ever eaten, and that his soul has grown thin under the burthen.

A commonplace about men of genius is that they usually have religious dispositions. It would be strange were it otherwise, seeing that genius is nothing but the power of discerning the things of the spirit. The first principle of the most recent form of "psychology" is, indeed, that there is no soul; but that man must have little genius who would not say "Amen" to St. Bernard's epigram, "He must have little spirit who thinks that a spirit is nothing."

After what has just been said, it seems paradoxical to be obliged to admit that the sins to which men of genius are usually most subject are those of sense. From pride, and its offspringenvy, hatred, and malice, which play so terrible a part in the affairs of most men, they are comparatively exempt. That they should often be more subject than others to be misled by the ease and pleasure of the senses may be because the senses of men of genius are more subtly permeated by the spirit, of which they are the ultimate life, than are those of the world at large, and are thereby rendered more acute and less sordidly wicked. This may be said, I hope, without in any way condoning error.

Men of genius, who are therewithal men of cultivated talents and great stores of appropriate information, are the only safe legislators and governors of empires; not only because theirs alone is the sufficiency of sound and far-seeing wisdom, but because they are far less likely than other men to be misled by personal motives and weak fears. But such men, unhappily, are the last to come to the front in states of ultra-popular government; and in such states they have accordingly to suffer that last misery (as by one of the greatest philosophers it has been called), the misery of being governed by worse men than themselves.

IV

POSSIBILITIES AND PERFORMANCES

IF we take stock of the world's actual achievements—intellectual, moral, and artistic—in the six thousand years during which we know anything about it, it is impossible not to be struck with the extreme smallness of the sum of the acquisitions and attainments of the human race which can bear any comparison with its desires and apparent possibilities. If those desires and possibilities had in no instances been fulfilled, the entire absence of attainment would have been less startling than is its actual paucity. It would not have been nearly so wonderful if none had reached the high table-lands of excellence in any department of human activity, as it is that those heights have been reached by some and by so few. And the marvel of this paucity becomes yet further increased when it is considered that not only is it all that mankind has done, but in all likelihood nearly as much as it could have done had it tried ever so hard. For it is a peculiarity of the very highest work in every kind, that it is not the result of painful labour, but that it is easier to do it than not to do it, when it can be done at all. So that humanity must not be allowed to cover its enormous shortcomings with an "I could an' I would." How many philosophers has philosophy produced? If Aristotle be the type, where is the other specimen of the species? How many statesmen have there been whose faculties and characters, nearly inspected, do not provoke the exclamation, "With how little wisdom the world is governed!" In how many Christians has Christianity flowered, as in the souls of St. John and St. Francis? Greek architecture and Greek sculpture mean little more than the Parthenon and its friezes. What survives of Greek poetry will scarcely fill one bookshelf, and English poetry, which forms the greater part of the rest of the poetry of the human race, would rest easily on three. The building of the Middle Ages is nothing but the repetition of one inspiration, which would remain transmitted to us almost in its entirety were the Cathedral of Freiburg the only specimen left to us. A single gallery of the Vatican would provide wall-room sufficient for all the paintings of the world that are able to fill with satisfying peace the eye which has been educated by Botticelli, Luini, and Raphael. An ordinary life affords abundant leisure to take in all that two hundred generations of mankind have so done as to fill the craving for what all men feel to be alone satisfyingly human. That is to say, one man in twenty millions or so has been able, during some—often very small—proportion of his life, to be and to do that which all men, when they behold such being and doing, feel to be their natural though utterly unattainable prerogative. Thousands and thousands climb, with praiseworthy struggles and integrity of purpose and with shouts of "Excelsior!" the minor peaks of life; while two or three in a generation are seen walking with easy breath about those great and tranquil table-lands for which all of us, on beholding them, feel that we were born. It is not that, in a world of inequalities, some two or three in a generation must naturally stand higher than all the rest, as only one among many competitors can be Senior Wrangler. That fuller excellence is a region, and not a pinnacle; and those who reach it are all upon a great and facile equality, their altitude being simply that of right and unhindered human faculty.

Every individual of the human race is, in this regard, an image of the race itself. Only for afew hours, perhaps, of the million which is about the sum of the longest lifetime, has each one easily and unaccountably found himself to be living indeed. Some accident, some passing occasion which has called upon him to be more than himself, some glimpse of grace in nature or in woman, some lucky disaster even, or some mere wayward tide of existence, has caused the black walls of his prison-house to vanish; and he has breathed in a realm of vision, generosity, and gracious peace, "too transient for delight and too divine." These prophetic moments—one in a million—pass; but, unless he has despised and denied them, they leave him capable, more or less, of understanding prophecy; and he knows that in him also there is a potentiality, realisable perhaps under other than present conditions, of becoming one in that great society in which such states of life appear to be not momentary crises but habits. The wider and the deeper his personal experience of beauty and felicity, the more readily will a man confess that life contains scarcely anything for fruition but abundance for hope; and the better he is acquainted with that which has been best done and said in all ages, the less he will be inclined to believe that the world is making any advances towards the realisation of the promise which every age repeats. An enigma forwhich science has no key is the certain fact, that if the world be not a prophecy of good things which it shows no likelihood of providing, then it is all nothing but a purposeless and badly conceived tragedy, upon which the sooner the black curtain drops the better. For if the world be not such a prophecy, then the best of men are of all men the most miserable; to these is given beyond others the "transitory gleam" which shows the dulness of their ordinary life for the lingering death it really is; but, knowing little or nothing of life as it is known to such, the stupid and "the wicked have no bonds in their death," and can only feel the comparatively tolerable evils of external and accidental adversity.

There never was a time in which the "higher life," "high art," etc., were less known than in the present, when every goose is gabbling about them. The proof is in the way these names are constantly associated with that of "progress"; whereas progress, as respects the realities, is, if it exists at all, most certainly a progress backwards. The rejoicings of Lord Macaulay and his like over the recent advances of mankind are exactly those of a prosperous shopman over the increase of his business; and the hallelujahs of science are mainly over the elaboration of mighty means for petty ends and of theories which explain awayGod and exhibit all that past ages have called wisdom as folly. It is too absurd! Yet we must not allow the present eclipse of the electric lights of true learning by the flaring tar-barrels of jubilant ignorance to discourage us in the belief that there is, on the whole, no cessation of the work for which the world goes on. The conscience of mankind, though occasionally confused and obscured, will always cry "Amen" to the great word of St. Augustine, "What ought to be must be;" and the rare achievements of genius and sanctity and the few and far-between glimpses of the life that is indeed life, which are accorded to all, will continue to be accepted as "the substance of things hoped for, the evidence of things not seen."

V

CHEERFULNESS IN LIFE AND ART

"REJOICE always: and again I say, Rejoice," says one of the highest authorities; and a poet who is scarcely less infallible in psychological science writes—

A cheerful heart is what the Muses love.

Dante makes Melancholy dismally punished in Purgatory; though his own interior gaiety—of which a word by and by—is so interior, and its outward aspect often so grim, that he is vulgarly considered to have himself been a sinner in this sort. Good art is nothing but a representation of life; and that the good are gay is a commonplace, and one which, strange to say, is as generally disbelieved as it is, when rightly understood, undeniably true. The good and brave heart is always gay in this sense: that, although it may be afflicted and oppressed by its own misfortunes and those of others, it refuses in the darkest moment to consent to despondency; and thus a habit of mind is formed which can discern in most of its own afflictions some cause for grave rejoicing, and can thence infer at least a probability of such cause in cases where it cannot be discerned. Regarding thus cheerfully and hopefully its own sorrows, it is not over-troubled by those of others, however tender and helpful its sympathies may be. It is impossible to weep much for that in others which we should smile at in ourselves; and when we see a soul writhing like a worm under what seems to us a small misfortune, our pity for its misery is much mitigated by contempt for its cowardice.

A couple of generations ago most people would have opened their eyes wide at any one who should have thought remarks like these worth making. Such truth formed part of the universal tradition of civilisation and moral culture. But a wilful melancholy, and, the twin sign of corruption, a levity which acutely fears and sympathises with pains which are literally only skin-deep, have been increasing upon us of late in a most portentous way. The much-vaunted growth of "humanity" has been due rather to a softening of the brain than of the heart. Huge moral ill, the fact of national degradation, the prospect of national disaster, arouses less pain in the sympathetic hearts of humanitarians than the yelp of a poodle whichhas had its ear pinched. Men and times do not talk about the virtues they possess. Which is more inhuman: to punish with rack and wheel the treason which voluntarily sacrifices or jeopardises the welfare of millions, or to condone or ignore it for the sake of momentary ease? The England in which melancholy and levity are becoming prevalent habits is merry England no more. "The nation thou hast multiplied, but not increased the joy." And we are not the only nation which deserves this lamentation of the prophet. The growths of melancholy and levity have been still more marked in France. In America, some traveller has remarked, "there is comfort everywhere, but no joy." America is accordingly the only country which has no art.

It is, as we have said, a vulgar error to consider Dante a melancholy poet. In the whole range of art, joy is nowhere expressed so often and with such piercing sweetness as in the *Paradiso*; and it flashes occasionally through the dun atmosphere of the other parts of the poem. The *Inferno* is pervaded by the vigorous joy of the poet at beholding thoroughly bad people getting their deserts; and the penances of purgatory are contemplated by him with the grave pleasure which is often felt by the saner sort of persons, even in this world, under the sufferingsthey acknowledge to be the appropriate punishment of and purification from the sins they have fallen into. Shakespeare is the most cheerful of poets. We read his deepest tragedies without contracting even a momentary stain of melancholy, however many tears they may have drawn from us. Calderon flies among horrors and disasters on the wings of a bird of Paradise, without any resulting incongruity; and like things may be said of the greatest painters and musicians, until quite recent times. But since about the beginning of this century how many of our geniuses have mingled their songs with tears and sighs over "insoluble problems" and "mysteries of life" which have no existence for a man who is in his right senses and who minds his own business; while the "scrannel pipes" of the smaller wits have been playing to the sorry Yankee tune of "There's nothing new, and there's nothing true, and it doesn't signify." Music has taken to imitate the wailing of lost spirits or the liveliness of the casino; and the highest ambition of several of our best painters seems to have been to evoke a pathos from eternal gloom.

This is false art, and represents a false life, or rather that which is not life at all; for life is not only joyful, it is joy itself. Life, unhindered by the internal obstruction of vice or the outwardobscurations of pain, sorrow, and anxiety, is pure and simple joy; as we have most of us experienced during the few hours of our lives in which, the conscience being free, all bodily and external evils have been removed or at least quiescent. And, though these glimpses of perfect sunshine are few and far between, the joy of life will not be wholly obscured to us by any external evil—provided the breast is clear of remorse, envy, discontent, or any other habitually cherished sin. The opportunities and hindrances of joyful life are pretty fairly distributed among all classes and persons. God is just, and His mercy is over all His works. If gardens and parks are denied to the inhabitant of a city lane, his eye is so sharpened by its fasts that it can drink in its full share of the sweetness of nature from a flowering geranium or a pot of crocuses on his window-sill. There are really very few persons who have not enough to eat. Marriage is open almost equally to all, except, perhaps, the less wealthy members of the upper orders. None are without opportunities of joy and abundant reasons for gratitude: and the hindrances of joy are, if justly considered, only opportunities of acquiring new capacities for delight. In proportion as life becomes high and pure it becomes gay. The profound spiritualities of the Greek and Indian myths laugh for joy; and there are, perhaps, no passages of Scripture more fondly dwelt upon in the Roman Breviary than those which paint the gladness of the Uncreated Wisdom: "When he balanced the foundations of the earth, I was with him, forming all things: and was delighted every day, playing before him at all times, playing in the world: and my delight is to be with the children of men."

VI

THE POINT OF REST IN ART

COLERIDGE, who had little technical knowledge of any art but that in which, when he was himself, he supremely excelled—poetry—had nevertheless a deeper insight into the fundamental principles of art than any modern writer, with the sole exception of Goethe. And this is one of his many fruitful sayings: "All harmony is founded on a relation to rest—on relative rest. Take a metallic plate and strew sand on it, sound an harmonic chord over the sand, and the grains will whirl about in circles and other geometrical figures, all, as it were, depending on some point of sand relatively at rest. Sound a discord, and every grain will whisk about without any order at all, in no figures, and with no point of rest."

Without pretending to be able to trace this principle of rest to more than a very limited distance, and in a very few examples, I think it is worth notice in a time when art generally is characterised by a want of that repose which until recent times has especially "marked the manners of the great." Look through the National Gallery, and few pictures will be found which would not add a grace of peace to the house they were hung in, no matter how wild the subject or passionate the motive. Step into an Academy Exhibition, and there will scarcely be discovered a dozen canvases in a thousand which, however skilful and in many respects admirable they may be, would not constitute points of *un*rest, if they were in daily and hourly sight. It is the same with nearly all modern poetry, sculpture, and architecture; and if it is not true of music, it is because music absolutely cannot exist without some reference to a point or points of rest, in keynote, fundamental strain, or reiterated refrain.

It might at first be supposed that, in a picture, this point should be that on which the eye should repose in order to bring the remainder into focal proportion; and this is true with regard to those painters who paint on the theory that the eye is fixed, and not roving in its regard. But this theory has never been that of the greatest times of art. Crome, Constable, and Gainsborough's landscapes do not fade off from a certain point on which the eye is supposed to be fixed; yet there will usually be found some point, generally quite insignificant in matter, on which, indeed, the eye does not necessarily fix itself, but to which it involuntarily returns for repose.

The most noteworthy remark to be made about this point of rest is, that it is not in itself the most but the least interesting point in the whole work. It is the *punctum indifferens* to which all that is interesting is more or less unconsciously referred. In an elaborate landscape it may be—as it is in one of Constable's—the sawn-off end of a branch of a tree: or a piece of its root, as it is in one of Michael Angelo's pieces in the Sistine Chapel. In the Dresden "Madonna" of Raphael it is the heel of the Infant. No one who has not given some thought to the subject can have any idea of the value of these apparently insignificant points in the pictures in which they occur, unless he tries the experiment of doing away with them. Cover them from sight and, to a moderately sensitive and cultivated eye, the whole life of the picture will be found to have been lowered.

In proportion to the extent and variety of points of interest in a painting or a poem the necessity for this point of rest seems to increase. In a lyric or idyll, or a painting with very few details, there is little need for it. It is accordingly in the most elaborate plays of Shakespeare that we findthis device in its fullest value; and it is from two or three of these that we shall draw our main illustrations of a little-noticed but very important principle of art. In *King Lear* it is by the character of Kent, in *Romeo and Juliet* by Friar Laurence, in *Hamlet* by Horatio, in *Othello* by Cassio, and in the *Merchant of Venice* by Bassanio, that the point of rest is supplied; and this point being also in each case a point of vital comparison by which we measure and feel the relationships of all the other characters, it becomes an element of far higher value than when it is simply an, as it were, accidental point of repose, like the lopped branch in Constable's landscape. Each of these five characters stands out of the stream of the main interest, and is additionally unimpressive in itself by reason of its absolute conformity to reason and moral order from which every other character in the play departs more or less. Thus Horatio is the exact *punctum indifferens* between the opposite excesses of the characters of Hamlet and Laertes—over-reasoning inaction and unreasoning action—between which extremes the whole interest of the play vibrates. The unobtrusive character of Kent is, as it were, the eye of the tragic storm which rages round it; and the departure, in various directions, of every character more or less frommoderation, rectitude, or sanity, is the more clearly understood or felt from our more or less conscious reference to him. So with the central and comparatively unimpressive characters in many other plays—characters unimpressive on account of their facing the exciting and trying circumstances of the drama with the regard of pure reason, justice, and virtue. Each of these characters is a peaceful focus radiating the calm of moral solution throughout all the difficulties and disasters of surrounding fate: a vital centre, which, like that of a great wheel, has little motion in itself, but which at once transmits and controls the fierce revolution of the circumference.

It is obvious, as I have indicated, that a point of rest and comparison is necessary only when the objects and interests are many and more or less conflicting; but the principle is sometimes at play in forms and works in which we should scarcely have expected to find it. An armlet, or even a finger-ring, gives every portion of the nude figure an increase of animation, unity, and repose. The artistic justification of the unmeaning "burthen" of many an old ballad may probably be found, at least in part, in the same principle; as may also be that of the trick—as old as poetry—of occasionally repeating a line or phrase without any apparent purpose in the repetition.

Of course the "point of rest" will not create harmony where—as in most modern works—its elements are absent; but, where harmony exists, it will be strangely brought out and accentuated by this in itself often trifling, and sometimes, perhaps, even accidental accessory.

VII

IMAGINATION

THERE are things which can never be more than approximately defined, and which, even when so defined, are only to be rightly understood in proportion to the degrees in which they are possessed by those who would attempt to comprehend them. Such are, for example, "imagination" and "genius"; which, being faculties that are possessed in a very low degree by nearly all and in a very high degree by extremely few, are matters of the most general interest and the most variable apprehension. That such faculties should, however, as far as possible, be understood is of great practical importance to all persons; inasmuch as it greatly concerns all to know something of the signs, sanctions, and claims of those powers by which they are inevitably more or less ruled, externally and internally.

It is nothing against a definition of an entity which cannot be fully defined to say that such definition is "new." It was objected against an interpretation by St. Augustine of some Old Testament history or parable, that other authorities had given other interpretations. "The more interpretations the better," was the saint's reply. In such cases various definitions and interpretations are merely apprehensions of various sides of a matter not wholly to be embraced or comprehended by any single definition or interpretation. In recent times genius and imagination have come to be widely regarded as one and the same thing. They are not so, however, though they are perhaps indissolubly connected. The most peculiar and characteristic mark of genius is insight into subjects which are dark to ordinary vision and for which ordinary language has no adequate expression. Imagination is rather the language of genius: the power which traverses at a single glance the whole external universe, and seizes on the likenesses and images, and their combinations, which are best able to embody ideas and feelings which are otherwise inexpressible; so that the "things which are unseen are known by the things which are seen." Imagination, in its higher developments, is so quick and subtle a power that the most delicate analysis can scarcely follow its shortest flights. Coleridge said that it would take a whole volume to analyse the effect of a certain passage of only a few syllables in length. In dealing with such a work as *The Tempest* criticism is absolutely helpless, and its noblest function is to declare its own helplessness by directing attention to beauty beyond beauty which defies analysis. *The Tempest*, like all very great works of art, is the shortest and simplest, and indeed the only possible expression of its "idea." The idea is the product of genius proper; the expression is the work of imagination. There are cases, however, in which it is hard to distinguish at all between these inseparable qualities. The initiation of a scientific theory seems often to have been due to the action of the imagination working independently of any peculiar direct insight; the analogy-discovering faculty—that is, the imagination—finding a law for a whole sphere of unexplained phenomena in the likeness of such phenomena to others of a different sphere of which the law is known. Hence the real discoverers of such theories are scarcely ever those who have obtained the credit of them; for nothing is usually more abhorrent to men of extraordinary imagination than "fact-grinding." Such men, after having flung out their discoveries to the contempt or neglect of their contemporaries, leave the future proof of them to mental mechanics; religiouslyavoiding such work themselves, lest, as Goethe said of himself, they should find themselves imprisoned in "the charnel-house of science." Genius and imagination of a very high kind are not at all uncommon in children under twelve years of age, especially when their education has been "neglected." The writer can guarantee the following facts from personal witness: A clever child of seven, who could not read, and had certainly never heard of the Newtonian theory of gravitation, said to his mother suddenly, "What makes this ball drop when I leave hold of it?—Oh, I know: the ground pulls it." Another child, a year or two older, lay stretched on a gravel path, staring intently on the pebbles. "They are alive," he cried, in the writer's hearing; "they are always wanting to burst, but something draws them in." This infantine rediscovery of the doctrine of the coinherence of attraction and repulsion in matter seems to have been an effort of direct insight. The repetition of the Newtonian apple revelation seems rather to have been the work of the imagination, tracking likeness in difference; but to discern such likeness is, again, an effort of direct insight, and justifies Aristotle's saying that this power of finding similitude in things diverse is a proof of the highest human faculty, and that thence poetry is worthier thanhistory. The poet's eye glances from heaven to earth, from earth to heaven; and his faculty of discerning likeness in difference enables him to express the unknown in the terms of the known, so as to confer upon the former a *sensible* credibility, and to give the latter a truly sacramental dignity. The soul contains world upon world of the most real of realities of which it has no consciousness until it is awakened to their existence by some parable or metaphor, some strain of rhythm or music, some combination of form or colour, some scene of beauty or sublimity, which suddenly expresses the inexpressible by a lower likeness. The vulgar cynic, blessing when he only means to bray, declares that love between the sexes is "all imagination." What can be truer? What baser thing is there than such love, when it is not of imagination all compact? or what more nearly divine when it is? Why? Because the imagination deals with the spiritual realities to which the material realities correspond, and of which they are only, as it were, the ultimate and sensible expressions. And here it may be noted, by the way, that Nature supplies the ultimate analogue of every divine mystery with some vulgar use or circumstance, in order, as it would seem, to enable the stupid and the gross to deny the divine without actual blasphemy.

Profligacy and "fact-grinding" destroy the imagination by habitually dwelling in ultimate expressions while denying or forgetting the primary realities of which they are properly only the vessels. Purity ends by finding a goddess where impurity concludes by confessing carrion. Which of these is the reality let each man judge according to his taste. "Fact-grinding"—which Darwin confessed and lamented had destroyed his imagination and caused him to "nauseate Shakespeare"—commonly ends in destroying the religious faculty, as profligacy destroys the faculty of love; for neither love nor religion can survive without imagination, which Shelley, in one of his prefaces, identifying genius with imagination, declares to be the power of discerning spiritual facts. Those who have no imagination regard it as all one with "fancy," which is only a playful mockery of imagination, bringing together things in which there is nothing but an accidental similarity in externals.

VIII

PATHOS

NEITHER Aristotle nor Hegel, the two great expositors of the relation of the emotions to art, has discussed the nature of that which is understood by moderns as "pathos." Aristotle has described in his *Rhetoric*, with the greatest acuteness and sensibility, the conditions and modes of exciting pity. But pity includes much that is excluded by pathos; and it may be useful to endeavour to ascertain what the limitations of the latter are, and what are its conditions in relation more particularly to art, in which it plays so important a part.

Pity, then, differs from pathos in this: the latter is simply emotional, and reaches no higher than the sensitive nature; though the sensitive nature, being dependent for its power and delicacy very much upon the cultivation of will and intellect, may be indefinitely developed by these activefactors of the soul. Pity is helpful, and is not deadened or repelled by circumstances which disgust the simply sensitive nature; and its ardour so far consumes such obstacles to merely emotional sympathy, that the person who truly pities finds the field of pathos extended far beyond the ordinary limits of the dainty passion which gives tears to the eyes of the selfish as well as the self-sacrificing. In an ideally perfect nature, indeed, pity and pathos, which is the feeling of pity, would be coextensive; and the latter would demand for its condition the existence of the former, with some ground of actual reality to work beneficially upon. On the other hand, entire selfishness would destroy even the faintest capacity for discerning pathos in art or circumstance. In the great mass of men and women there is sufficient virtue of pity—pity that would act if it had the opportunity—to extend in them the *feeling* of pity, that is pathos, to a far larger range of circumstances than their active virtue would be competent to encounter, even if it had the chance.

Suffering is of itself enough to stir pity; for absolute wickedness, with the torment of which all wholesome minds would be quite content, cannot be certainly predicated of any individual sufferer; but pathos, whether in a drawing-room tale of delicate distress or in a tragedy of Æschylusor Shakespeare, requires that some obvious goodness, or beauty, or innocence, or heroism should be the subject of suffering, and that the circumstance or narration of it should have certain conditions of repose, contrast, and form. The range of pathos is immense, extending from the immolation of an

Isaac or an Iphigenia to the death of a kitten that purrs and licks the hand about to drown it. Next to the fact of goodness, beauty, innocence, or heroism in the sufferer, contrast is the chief factor in artistic pathos. The celestial sadness of Desdemona's death is immensely heightened by the black shadow of Iago; and perhaps the most intense touch of pathos in all history is that of Gordon murdered at Khartoum, while his betrayer occupies himself, between the acts of a comedy at the Criterion, in devising how best he may excuse his presence there by denying that he was aware of the *contretemps* or by representing his news of it as non-official. The singer of Fair Rosamund's sorrows knew the value of contrast when he sang—

Hard was the heart that gave the blow,
Soft were the lips that bled.

Every one knows how irresistible are a pretty woman's tears.

Nought is there under heav'n's wide hollowness
That moves more dear compassion of mind
Than beauty brought to unworthy wretchedness.

It is partly the contrast of beauty, which is the natural appanage of happiness, that renders her tears so pathetic; but it is still more the way in which she is given to smiling through them. The author of the *Rhetoric* shows his usual incomparable subtilty of observation when he notes that a little good coming upon or in the midst of extremity of evil is a source of the sharpest pathos; and when the shaft of a passionate female sorrow is feathered with beauty and pointed with a smile there is no heart that can refuse her her will. In absolute and uncontrolled suffering there is no pathos. Nothing in the *Inferno* has this quality except the passage of Paolo and Francesca, still embracing, through the fiery drift. It is the embrace that makes the pathos, "tempering extremities with extreme sweet," or at least with the memory of it. Our present sorrows generally owe their grace of pathos to their "crown," which is "remembering happier things." No one weeps in sympathy with the "base self-pitying tears" of Thersites, or with those of any whose grief is without some contrasting dignity of curb. Even a little child does not move us by its sorrow, when expressed by tears and cries, a tenth part so muchas by the quivering lip of attempted self-control. A great and present evil, coupled with a distant and uncertain hope, is also a source of pathos; if indeed it be not the same with that which Aristotle describes as arising from the sequence of exceeding ill and a little good. There is pathos in a departing pleasure, however small. It is the fact of sunset, not its colours—which are the same as those of sunrise—that constitutes its sadness; and in mere darkness there may be fear and distress, but not pathos. There are few things so pathetic in literature as the story of the supper which Amelia, in Fielding's novel, had prepared for her husband, and to which he did not come, and that of Colonel Newcome becoming a Charterhouse pensioner. In each of these cases the pathos arises wholly from the contrast of noble reticence with a sorrow which has no direct expression. The same necessity for contrast renders reconciliations far more pathetic than quarrels, and the march to battle of an army to the sound of cheerful military music more able to draw tears than the spectacle of the battle itself.

The soul of pathos, like that of wit, is brevity. Very few writers are sufficiently aware of this. Humour is cumulative and diffusive, as Shakespeare, Rabelais, and Dickens well knew; but how many a good piece of pathos has been spoiled by the historian of Little Nell by an attempt to make too much of it! A drop of citric acid will give poignancy to a feast; but a draught of it——! Hence it is doubtful whether an English eye ever shed a tear over the *Vita Nuova*, whatever an Italian may have done. Next to the patient endurance of heroism, the bewilderment of weakness is the most fruitful source of pathos. Hence the exquisitely touching points in *A Pair of Blue Eyes, Two on a Tower, The Trumpet-Major*, and other of Hardy's novels.

Pathos is the luxury of grief, and when it ceases to be other than a keen-edged pleasure it ceases to be pathos. Hence Tennyson's question in "Love and Duty," "Shall sharpest pathos blight us?" involves a misunderstanding of the word; although his understanding of the thing is well proved by such lyrics as "Tears, idle tears," and "O well for the fisherman's boy." Pleasure and beauty—which may be said to be pleasure visible—are without their highest perfection if they are without a touch of pathos. This touch, indeed, accrues naturally to profound pleasure and to great beauty by the mere fact of the incongruity of their earthly surroundings and the sense of isolation, peril, and impermanence caused thereby. It is a doctrine of that inexhaustible and (except by Dante) almost unworked mine of poetry, Catholic theology, that the felicity of the angels and glorified saints and of God Himself would not be perfect without the edge of pathos, which it receives from the fall and reconciliation of man. Hence, on Holy Saturday the Church exclaims, "O felix culpa!" and hence "there is more joy in heaven over one sinner that repenteth than over ninety and nine righteous who need no repentance." Sin, says St. Augustine, is the necessary shadow of heaven; and pardon, says some other, is the highest light of its beatitude.

IX

POETICAL INTEGRITY

THE assertion that the value of the words of a poet does and ought to depend very much upon his personal character may seem, at the first glance, a violent paradox; but it is demonstrably true. A wise or tender phrase in the mouth of a Byron or a Moore will be despised, where a commonplace of morality or affection in that of a Wordsworth or a Burns is respected. If the author of *Don Juan* had said that for him "the meanest flower that blows could give thoughts that do often lie too deep for tears," as he would have said had it occurred to him to do so, no one would have believed him; it would have passed for a mere "poetical licence," and would have been excused as such and forgotten. Byron and Wordsworth have both declared in words of similar force and beauty that the sights and sounds of nature "haunted them like a passion." But the declaration was not consistent with what we know of Byron, and it was consistent with what we know of Wordsworth; and in the one case it creates a like frame of mind in the reader, while in the other it passes like a melodious wind, leaving no impression. Now this mighty element of character resides, not in the poet's active life, by which he is and ought to be socially judged; but in the spiritual consistency and integrity of his mind and heart, as it is to be inferred from the cumulative testimony of his words, which are, after all, the safest witnesses of what the man truly is. A man's actions—although we are bound socially to judge him thereby—may belie him: his words never. Out of his mouth shall the interior man be judged; for the interior man is what he heartily desires to be, however miserably he may fail to bring his external life into correspondence with his desire; and the words of the man will infallibly declare what he thus inwardly is, especially when, as in the case of the poet, the powers of language are so developed as to become the very glass of the soul, reflecting its purity and integrity, or its stains and insincerities, with a fidelity of which the writer himself is but imperfectly conscious.

To a soundly trained mind there is no surer sign of shallowness and of interior corruption than thathabitual predominance of form over formative energy, of splendour of language and imagery over human significance, which has so remarkably distinguished a great deal of the most widely praised poetry of the past eighty years. Much of this poetry has about as much relation to actual or imaginative reality as the transformation scene of a pantomime; and much more—called "descriptive"—has so low a degree of significance and betrays so inhuman an absorption in the merest superficies of nature, that when the writer pretends to deal with those facts and phenomena of humanity which, directly or indirectly, are the main region of every true poet's song, he has to overcome our sense that he is an habitual trifler before he can gain credit for sincerity, even when he is giving utterance to what may really be a passing strain of true poetic thought and feeling. A poet who is thus constantly occupied with the superficies of nature may probably attain to an accuracy and splendour of analytical description which has its value in its way, and which may, in certain transitory conditions of popular taste, raise him to the highest pinnacle of favour. But such poetry will be judged, in the end, by its human significance; and the writer of it will have the fatal verdict of "heartless" recorded against him—a verdict which even in the time of his favour is implicitlypronounced by the indifference with which his professions of human principle and feeling are received, even by his admirers.

The slightest touch of genuine humanity is of more actual and poetic value than all that is not human which the sun shines on. The interest of what is called "descriptive" or "representative" in real poetry and all real art is always human, or, in other words, "imaginative." A description by Wordsworth, Coleridge, or Burns, a landscape by Crome, Gainsborough, or Constable, is not merely nature, but nature reflected in and giving expression to a state of mind. The state of mind is the true subject, the natural phenomena the terms in which it is uttered; and there has never been a greater critical fallacy than that contained in Mr. Ruskin's strictures on the "pathetic fallacy." Nature has no beauty or pathos (using the term in its widest sense) but that with which the mind invests it. Without the imaginative eye it is like a flower in the dark, which is only beautiful as having in it a power of reflecting the colours of the light. The true light of nature is the human eye; and if the light of the human eye is darkness, as it is in those who see nothing but surfaces, how great is that darkness!

The saying of Wordsworth concerning the Poet, that

You must love him ere to you
He will seem worthy of your love,

which at first reading sounds very much like nonsense, is absolutely true. He must have won your credit and confidence in his words, by proofs of habitual veracity and sincerity, before you can so receive the words which come from his heart that they will move your own. If, in the utterance of what he offers to you as the cry or the deep longing of passion, you catch him in busily noticing trifles—for which very likely he gets praised for "accurate observation of nature"—you will put him down as one who knows nothing of the passion he is pretending to express. If you detect him in the endeavour to say "fine things" in order to win your admiration for himself, instead of rendering his whole utterance a single true thing, which shall win your sympathy with the thought or feeling by which he declares himself to be dominated, the result will be the same; as also it will be if you discover that the beauty of his words is obtained rather by the labour of polish than the inward labour and true finish of passion. When, on the other hand, some familiarity with the poet's work has assured you that, though his speech may be unequal and sometimes inadequate, it is never false; that he has always something to say, even when he fails in saying it: then you will not onlybelieve in and be moved by what he says well; but when the form is sometimes imperfect you will be carried over such passages, as over thin ice, by the formative power of passion or feeling which quickens the whole; although you would reject such passages with disgust were they found in the writing of a man in whose thoughts you know that the manner stands first and the matter second.

X

THE POETRY OF NEGATION

POETRY is essentially catholic and affirmative, dealing only with the permanent facts of nature and humanity, and interested in the events and controversies of its own time only so far as they evolve manifestly abiding fruits. But the abiding fruits of such events and controversies are very rarely manifest until the turmoil in which they are produced has long since subsided; and therefore poets, in all times before our own, have either allowed the present to drift unheeded by or have so handled its phenomena as to make them wholly subsidiary to and illustrative of matters of well-ascertained stability. The many occasional poems of past times, of which temporary incidents have been the subjects, in no way contradict this assertion in the main; and the casual example of a poet like Dryden affords only the confirming exception. Dryden was fond of protesting, especially when he was a Catholic; and there is no doubt but that this habit added greatly to his popularity in his lifetime, as it does to the favour in which some of the most distinguished of our modern poets are now held; but all those points which probably constituted the high lights of Dryden's poetry to his contemporaries have suffered in course of time a change like that which has come over the whites of many of Sir Joshua Reynolds' pictures; and it is much to be feared that a similar fate awaits a large proportion of what has been written by several of the best poets of the generation which is now passing away. Most of our recent poets, even while condemning political revolution, have shared in the ideas or feelings which are at the bottom of revolutions, a hope which the facts of nature do not justify, and a disbelief in what those facts do justify—namely, the ineradicable character of moral evil, with its circumstantial consequences. The heart of the modern poet is, as a rule, always vibrating between the extremes of despondent grumbling at the present conditions and hasty and unreasonable aspirations for the improvement of his kind; his tragedies and hymns of rejoicing are alike void of the dignity and repose which arise from a sound confession of the facts of humanity and a cheerful resignation to its imperfections; and he whose true function is to stand aside as the tranquil seer too often now becomes the excited agent in matters which concern him least of all men, because of all men he is the least fitted to meddle with them. It is hard to say which is more wonderful—the clearness of the true poet's vision for things when he is contented with looking at them as they are, or his blindness when he fancies he can mend them. Famous statesmen have marvellously drivelled in verse, but not more marvellously than famous poets have drivelled in what pertains to statesmanship. It is scarcely without a feeling of amazement that a man of ordinary good sense contrasts the power of poetic vision in writers like Victor Hugo and Carlyle with the childishness of their judgments when they propose antidotes for evils which they so clearly see, but for which they do not see that there are no antidotes, but only palliatives. Looking for what they fancy may be, when their vocation is to proclaim with clearness that which is, one poet will shriek to us (for untruths cannot be sung) that all will be well when King Log is down and King Stork reigns in his stead; another that Niagara may yet be dammed if country gentlemen will hire drill-sergeants to put their gardeners and farm-labourers through the goose-step; another says the world will be saved if a few gentlemen and ladies, with nothing better to do, will take to playing at being their own domestics; a fourth, in order to save morals, proposes their abolition; a fifth proclaims that all will have good wages when there remains no one to pay them; a sixth discovers in the science of the future a sedative for human passions instead of a wider platform for their display; and so on. Others, who have no patent medicines on hand, impotently grumble or rage at evils in which, if they looked steadily, they might discern the good of justice, or that of trial, or both (as great poets in past times always have done); and, instead of truly singing, they sob hysterical sympathy with such sufferings in others as, if they were their own, they either would bear or know that they ought to bear with equanimity.

The statesman, the social reformer, the political economist, the natural philosopher, the alms-giver, the hospital visitor, the preacher, even the cynical humorist, has each his function, and each is rightly more or less negative; but the function of the poet is clearly distinguished from all of these, and is higher though less obtrusive than any. It is simply affirmative of things which it greatly concerns men to know, but which they have either not discovered or have allowed to lapse into the death of commonplace. He alone has the power of revealing by his insight and magic words theundreamt-of mines of felicity which exist potentially for all in social relationships and affections. The inexhaustible glories of nature are a blank for many who are yet able to behold them reflected in his perceptions. His convincing song can persuade many to believe in, if they do not attain to taste—as he, if indeed he be a poet, must have tasted—the sweet and wholesome kernel which the rough shell of unmerited suffering conceals for those who are patient. And he can so contemplate the one real evil in the world as to give body and life and intelligibility to that last and sharpest cry of faith, "O felix culpa!"

The temptations which our time offers to the poet in order to induce him to forsake his own line are very great, and poets are human. The conceited present craves to have singers of its own, who will praise it, or at least abuse it; and it pays them well for pandering to its self-consciousness, lavishing its best honours upon them as leaders of the "Liberal movement," and scoffing at those, as "behind their time," who stand apart and watch and help those abiding developments of humanity which advance "with the slow process of the suns."

XI

THE LIMITATIONS OF GENIUS

IN art, as in higher matters, "strait is the gate, and narrow is the way, which leadeth unto life, and few there be that find it;" and the initial cause of failure, in many who seem to have faculties which should ensure success, is not so much the difficulty of the road which leads to it, as want of humility in confessing its narrowness. Each man is by birth a unique individuality, which the circumstances of his life will increase and develop continually, if he be content to do his duty in the station, intellectual and otherwise, to which it has pleased God to call him, without falling below its obligations or assuming others which have not been laid upon him. The low but still priceless degree of genius which consists in individuality in manners, and which renders the possessor of it powerfully though imperceptibly edifying in all companies, is open to all, though few are sufficiently simple and honest andunambitious to attain to it, by turning neither to the right hand nor the left in pursuit of their particular good of life.

"Originality," whether in manners, action, or art, consists simply in a man's being upon his own line; in his advancing with a single mind towards his unique apprehension of good; and in his doing so in harmony with the universal laws which secure to all men the liberty of doing as he is doing, without hindrance from his or any other's individuality. Unless "originality" thus works in submission to and harmony with general law, it loses its nature. In morals it becomes sin or insanity, in manners and in art oddity and eccentricity, which are in reality the extreme opposites and travesties of originality. As in religion it is said that "no man can know whether he is worthy of love," so in art and ordinary life no man can know whether he is original. If through habitual fidelity to his idea of good he has attained to originality, he will be the last person in the world to know it. If he thinks he is original, he is probably not so; and if he is commonly praised for originality, he may hardly hope to attain to any such distinction. Originality never expresses itself in harsh and obtrusive singularities. A society of persons of true originality in manners would be like an oak-tree, the leaves of which alllook alike until they are carefully compared, when it is found that they are all different. In art, the sphere of extraordinary originalities, there is the same absence of strongly pronounced distinctions, and therefore the same withdrawal from the recognition of the vulgar, who look for originality in antics, oddities, crudities, and incessant violations of the universal laws, which true originality religiously observes; its very function consisting, as it does, in upholding those laws and illustrating them and making them unprecedentedly attractive by its own peculiar emphases and modulations.

The individuality or "genius" of a man, which results from fidelity in life and art to his "ruling love," is almost necessarily narrow. Shakespeare is the only artist that ever lived whose genius has even approached to universality. His range is so great that ordinary readers, if, like Mr. Frederic Harrison, they had the courage to speak their impressions, would with him condemn the greater part of his work as "rubbish"—that is, as having no counterpart in the "positivism" of their actual or imaginative experience. Every play of Shakespeare is a new vision—not only a new aspect of his vision, as is the case with the different works of nearly all other artists, even the greatest. Narrowness, indeed, so far from being opposed togreatness in art, is often its condition. Dante and Wordsworth are proofs that greatness of genius consists in seeing clearly rather than much; and well it would have been both for poets and for readers had the former always or even generally understood the economy of moving always on their own lines. Nothing has so much injured modern art as the artist's ambition to show off his "breadth"; and many an immortal lyric or idyll has been lost because the lyric or idyllic poet has chosen to forsake his line for the production of exceedingly mortal epics or tragedies. The modern custom of exhibiting all the works of a single painter at a time affords proof which every one will understand of what has been said. Who, with an eye for each painter's true quality, can have gone over the collections in recent years of the pictures of Landseer, Reynolds, Rossetti, Blake, Holman Hunt, and others, without a feeling of surprise, and some perhaps irrational disappointment, at the discovery for the first time of the artist's limitations? Each had painted the same vision over and over again! There was no harm in that. The mistake was in bringing together the replicas which should have adorned "palace chambers far apart." But poets, whose "works" are always collectively exhibited, should beware how they betray the inevitable fact of the narrowness of genius. Not only should theynever leave their own line for another which is not their own, but they should be equally careful not to go over it again when they have once got to the end of it.

XII

LOVE AND POETRY

EVERY man and woman who has not denied or falsified nature knows, or at any rate feels, that love, though the least "serious," is the most significant of all things. The wise do not talk much about this knowledge, for fear of exposing its delicate edge to the stolid resistance of the profligate and unbelieving, and because its light, though, and for the reason that, it exceeds all other, is deficient in definition. But they see that to this momentary transfiguration of life all that is best in them looks forward or looks back, and that it is for this the race exists, and not this for the race— the seed for the flower, not the flower for the seed. All religions have sanctified this love, and have found in it their one word for and image of their fondest and highest hopes; and the Catholic has exalted it into a "great Sacrament," holding that, with Transubstantiation—which itresembles—it is only unreasonable because it is above reason. "The love which is the best ground of marriage," writes also the Protestant and "judicious" Hooker, "is that which is least able to render a reason for itself." Indeed, the extreme unreasonableness of this passion, which gives cause for so much blaspheming to the foolish, is one of its surest sanctions and a main cause of its inexhaustible interest and power; for who but a "scientist" values greatly or is greatly moved by anything he can understand—that which can be comprehended being necessarily less than we are ourselves?

In this matter the true poet must always be a mystic—altogether to the vulgar, and more or less to all who have not attained to his peculiar knowledge. For what is a mystery but that which one does not know? The common handicrafts used to be called mysteries; and their professors were mystics to outsiders exactly in the sense that poets or theologians, with sure, but to them uncommunicated and perhaps incommunicable, knowledge, are mystics to the many. The poet simply knows more than they do; but it flatters their malignant vanity to call him names which they mean to be opprobrious, though they are not, because he is not such a spiritual pauper as themselves. But poets are mystics,not only by virtue of knowledge which the greater part of mankind does not possess, but also because they deal with knowledge against which the accusation of dunces who know the differential calculus is etymologically true—namely, that it is *absurd*. Love is eternally absurd, for that which is the root of all things must itself be without root. Aristotle says that things are unintelligible to man in proportion as they are simple; and another says, in speaking of the mysteries of love, that the angels themselves desire in vain to look into these things.

In the hands of the poet mystery does not hide knowledge, but reveals it as by its proper medium. Parables and symbols are the only possible modes of expressing realities which are clear to perception though dark to the understanding. "Without a parable he spake not" who always spake of primary realities. Every spiritual reality fades into something else, and none can tell the point at which it fades. The only perfectly definite things in the universe are the conceptions of a fool, who would deny the sun he lives by if he could not see its disk. Natural sciences are definite, because they deal with laws which are not realities but conditions of realities. The greatest and perhaps the only real use of natural science is to supply similes and parables for poets and theologians.

But if the realities of love were not in themselves dark to the understanding, it would be necessary to darken them—not only lest they should be profaned, but also because, as St. Bernard says, "The more the realities of heaven are clothed with obscurity, the more they delight and attract, and nothing so much heightens longing as such tender refusal." "Night," says the inspirer of St. Bernard, "is the light of my pleasures."

Love is rooted deeper in the earth than any other passion; and for that cause its head, like that of the Tree Igdrasil, soars higher into heaven. The heights demand and justify the depths, as giving them substance and credibility. "That He hath ascended—what is it but because He first also descended into the lower parts of the earth?" Love "reconciles the highest with the lowest, ordering all things strongly and sweetly from end to end." St. Bernard says that "divine love" (religion) "has its first root in the most secret of the human affections." This affection is the only key to the inner sanctuaries of that faith which declares, "Thy Maker is thy Husband;" the only clue by which searchers of the "secret of the King," in the otherwise inscrutable writings of prophet and apostle, discover, as Keble writes, "the loving hint that meets the longing guess," which looks to the future for the satisfying andabiding reality, the passage of whose momentary shadow forms the supreme glory of our mortality.

The whole of after-life depends very much upon how life's transient transfiguration in youth by love is subsequently regarded; and the greatest of all the functions of the poet is to aid in his readers the fulfilment of the cry, which is that of nature as well as religion, "Let not my heart forget the things mine eyes have seen." The greatest perversion of the poet's function is to falsify the memory of that transfiguration of the senses, and to make light of its sacramental character. This character is instantly recognised by the unvitiated heart and apprehension of every youth and maiden; but it is very easily forgotten and profaned by most, unless its sanctity is upheld by priests and poets. Poets are naturally its prophets—all the more powerful because, like the prophets of old, they are wholly independent of the priests, and are often the first to discover and rebuke the lifelessness into which that order is always tending to fall. If society is to survive its apparently impending dangers, it must be mainly by guarding and increasing the purity of the sources in which society begins. The world is finding out, as it has often done before, and more or less forgotten, that it cannot do without religion.Love is the first thing to wither under its loss. What love does in transfiguring life, that religion does in transfiguring love: as any one may see who compares one state or time with another. Love is sure to be something less than human if it is not something more; and the so-called extravagances of the youthful heart, which always claims a character for divinity in its emotions, fall necessarily into sordid, if not shameful, reaction, if those claims are not justified to the understanding by the faith which declares man and woman to be priest and priestess to each other of relations inherent in Divinity itself, and proclaimed in the words "Let us make man in our own image" and "male and female created he them." Nothing can reconcile the intimacies of love to the higher feelings, unless the parties to them are conscious—and true lovers always are—that, for the season at least, they justify the words "I have said, Ye are gods." Nuptial love bears the clearest marks of being nothing other than the rehearsal of a communion of a higher nature. Its felicity consists in a perpetual conversion of phase from desire to sacrifice, and from sacrifice to desire, accompanied by unchangeable complaisance in the delight shining in the beauty of the beloved; and it is agitated in all its changes by fear, without which love cannot long exist as emotion.Such a state, in proportion to its fervour, delicacy, and perfection, is ridiculous unless it is regarded as a "great sacrament." It is the inculcation of this significance which has made love between man and woman what it is now—at least to the idea and aspirations of all good minds. It is time that the sweet doctrine should be enforced more clearly. Love being much more respected and religion much less than of old, the danger of profanation is not so great as it was when religion was revered and love despised. The most characteristic virtue of woman, or at least the most alluring of her weaknesses—her not caring for masculine truth and worth unless they woo her with a smile or a touch or some such flattery of her senses—is the prevailing vice of most men, especially in these times. This general effeminacy is the poet's great opportunity. It is his pontifical privilege to feel the truth; and his function is to bridge the gulf between severe verity and its natural enemy, feminine sentiment, by speech which, without any sacrifice of the former, is "simple, sensuous, and passionate." He insinuates in nerve-convincing music the truths which the mass of mankind must feel before they believe. He leads them by their affections to things above their affections, making Urania acceptable to them by her prænomen Venus. He is the apostleof the Gentiles, and conveys to them, without any flavour of cant or exclusiveness, the graces which the chosen people have too often denied or disgraced in their eyes.

XIII

KEATS

MR. SIDNEY COLVIN'S book upon Keats is, in the main, a welcome exception to what has become, of late, the rule in this class of work. It is remarkably just, and every good reader will feel it to be the more warmly appreciative because it is scarcely ever extravagantly so. The bulk of Keats's poetry, including "Endymion," is estimated at its true worth, which, as Keats—the severest judge of his own work—knew and confessed, was not much; and the little volume (justly styled by Mr. Colvin "immortal") which was published in 1820, and which does not consist of more than about 3000 lines, is declared to contain nearly the whole of the poet's effective writing. And even in this little volume—which includes "Lamia," "Isabella," "The Eve of St. Agnes," the five "Odes," and "Hyperion"—Mr. Colvin acutely detects and boldly points out manyserious defects. From the comparatively worthless waste of the rest of Keats's writing, Mr. Colvin picks out with accurate discernment the few pieces and passages of real excellence; and he does criticism good service in directing attention to the especial value of the fragment called "The Eve of St. Mark," and of that which is probably the very finest lyric in the English language, "La Belle Dame sans Merci."

As long as Mr. Colvin limits himself to the positive beauties and defects of Keats's poetry he is nearly always right; it is only in his summing up and in his estimate of the comparative worth of his subject that a less enthusiastic critic must part company with him. "I think it probable that by power, as well as by temperament and aim, he was the most Shakespearian spirit that has lived since Shakespeare." Is not the truth rather that, among real poets, Keats was the most un-Shakespearian poet that ever lived? True poets may be divided into two distinct classes, though there is a border-line at which they occasionally become confused. In the first class, which contains all the greatest poets, with Shakespeare at their head, intellect predominates; governing and thereby strengthening passion, and evolving beauty and sweetness as accidents—though inevitable accidents—of its operation. The vision of suchpoets may almost be described in the words of St. Thomas Aquinas, in speaking of the Beatific Vision. "The vision," he writes, "is a virtue, the beatitude an accident." Such poets are truly spoken of as masculine. In the other class—in which Keats stands as high as any other, if not higher—the "beatitude," the beauty and sweetness, is the essential, the truth and power of intellect and passion the accident. These poets are, without any figure of speech, justly described as feminine (not necessarily effeminate); and they are separated from the first class by a distance as great as that which separates a truly manly man from a truly womanly woman. The trite saying that the spirit of the great poet has always a feminine element is perfectly true notwithstanding. "The man is not without the woman;" though "the man is not for the woman, but the woman for the man." The difference lies in that which has the lead and mastery. In Keats the man had not the mastery. For him a thing of beauty was not only a joy for ever, but was the supreme and only good he knew or cared to know; and the consequence is that his best poems are things of exquisite and most sensitively felt beauty, and nothing else. But it is a fact of primary significance, both in morals and in art (a fact which is sadly lost sight of just now), that the highestbeauty and joy are not attainable when they occupy the first place as motives, but only when they are more or less the accidents of the exercise of the manly virtue of the vision of truth. There is at fitting seasons a serene splendour and a sunny sweetness about that which is truly masculine, whether in character or in art, which women and womanly artists never attain—an inner radiance of original loveliness and joy which comes, and can only come, of the purity of motive which regards external beauty and delight as accidental.

In his individual criticisms of Keats's poems Mr. Colvin fully recognises their defect of masculine character. In speaking of "Isabella" he says: "Its personages appeal to us, not so much humanly and in themselves, as by the circumstances, scenery, and atmosphere amidst which we see them move. Herein lies the strength, and also the weakness, of modern romance: its strength, inasmuch as the charm of the mediæval colour and mystery is unfailing for those who feel it at all; its weakness, inasmuch as under the influence of that charm both writer and reader are too apt to forget the need for human and moral truth; and without these no great literature can exist." Again: "In Keats's conceptions of his youthful heroes there is at all times a touch, not the wholesomest, of effeminacy and physical softness, and the influence of passionhe is apt to make fever and unman them quite; as, indeed, a helpless and enslaved submission of all the faculties to love proved, when it came to the trial, to be the weakness of his own nature." And again: "In matters of poetic feeling and fancy Keats and Hunt had not a little in common. Both alike were given to 'luxuriating' somewhat effusively and fondly over the 'deliciousness' of whatever they liked in art, books, and nature." In these and other equally just and unquestionable criticisms of Keats's character and works, surely Mr. Colvin sufficiently refutes his own assertion that this writer was "by temperament" "the most Shakespearian" of poets since Shakespeare. And whether he was also such (as Mr. Colvin further asserts him to have been) "by power," let the poet's work declare. In his own lovely line—which he faithfully kept to in "Lamia," "Isabella," "The Eve of St. Agnes," and the "Odes"—he is unsurpassed and perhaps unequalled. When he is true to that line we do not feel the want of anything better, though we may know that there is something better: as, in the presence of a beautiful woman, we do not sigh because she is not a General Gordon or a Sir Thomas More. But let Keats try to assume the man—as he does in his latest work, his attempts at dramatic composition or at satirical humour, in the "Cap and Bells"—and all his life and power seem to shrivel and die, like the beauty of Lamia in the presence of Apollonius. Some of his readers may object the semblance of Miltonic strength in certain passages of the fragment "Hyperion"; but Keats himself knew and admitted that it was only a semblance and an echo, and therefore wisely abandoned the attempt, having satisfied himself with having shown the world that there was no object of merely external nature, from "roses amorous of the moon" to

The solid roar
Of thunderous waterfalls and torrents hoarse,
Pouring a constant bulk, uncertain where,

which he had not nerves to feel and words so to utter that others should feel as he did.

In making this distinction between poetry of a masculine and that of a feminine order, it must be understood that no sort of disrespect is intended to the latter in saying a good word for that "once important sex" of poetry which the bewitching allurements of Keats and Shelley and their followers have caused, for a season, to be comparatively despised. The femininity of such poets as these is a glorious and immortal gift, such as no mortal lady has ever attained or ever will attain. It has been proved to us how well a mortal lady may become able to read the classics; but, humbled as some of us may feel by her having headed the Tripos, it is still some compensation for those of our sex to remember that we alone can write "classics," even of the feminine order. Nor let it be thought that we have been insisting upon a modern and fanciful distinction in thus dividing great men into two classes, in one of which the masculine and in the other the feminine predominates. It is a fact the observation of which is as old as the mythology which attributed the parentage of heroes in whom the intellectual powers prevailed to the union of gods with women, while those who distinguished themselves by more external and showy faculties were said to have been born of the commerce of goddesses with men.

XIV

WHAT SHELLEY WAS

PROFESSOR DOWDEN has had access to a very large quantity of hitherto unpublished correspondence and other matter, some of which throws much new light upon Shelley's singular character; and, but for one most important point—his sudden separation from Harriet Westbrook, for which no substantial reason is given—the Professor's eleven hundred closely printed pages contain all and more than all that any reasonable person can want to know about the subject. Professor Dowden's arrangement of this mass of material is so lucid that interest seldom flags; and the whole work reads like a first-class sensational novel, of which the only faults are that the characters are unnatural and the incidents improbable. A beautiful youth of almost superhuman genius, sensitiveness, and self-abnegation, is the hero. He is given early to blaspheming whateversociety has hitherto respected; and to cursing the King and his father—an old gentleman whose chief foible seems to have been attachment to the Church of England. His charity is so angelical that he remains on the best of terms with one man who has tried to seduce his wife, and with another—a beautiful young lord with a club-foot, whom he finds wallowing in a society given to vices which cannot be named, and who is also a supreme poet—notwithstanding the fact that this lord has had a child by one of the ladies of his (the hero's) wife's family and treats her with the most unmerited contempt and cruelty. He adores three really respectable and attractive young ladies—by name Harriet Westbrook, Elizabeth Hitchener, and Emilia Viviani—with a passion which eternity cannot exhaust, and praises them in music like that of the spheres (witness "Epipsychidion"); and, anon, Harriet is "a frantic idiot," Elizabeth a "brown demon," and Emilia a "centaur." "It was," says his biographer, "one of the infirmities of Shelley's character that, from thinking the best of a friend or acquaintance, he could of a sudden, and with insufficient cause, pass over to the other side and think the worst." It is, perhaps, fortunate that Providence should afflict supreme sanctities and geniuses with such "infirmities"; otherwise we might take them for something more than meresaints and poets. The hero, as became absolute charity, gave every one credit—at least, when it suited his mood and convenience—for being as charitable as himself: witness his soliciting Harriet Westbrook for money after he had run away with his fresh "wife," her rival. He was addicted even from his babyhood to the oddest and most "charming" eccentricities.

"When Bysshe," then quite a child, "one day set a fagot-stack on fire, the excuse was a charming one: he did so that he might have 'a little hell of his own.'" At Eton "in a paroxysm of rage he seized the nearest weapon, a fork, and stuck it into the hand of his tormentor." On another occasion, when his tutor found him apparently setting fire to himself and the house, and asked him "What on earth are you doing, Shelley?" he replied, "Please, sir, I'm raising the devil." The pet virtue of the hero was tolerance. "Here I swear," he writes to Mr. Hogg, "and as I break my oaths, may Infinity, Eternity blast me—here I swear that never will I forgive intolerance! It is the only point on which I allow myself to encourage revenge ... not one that leaves the wretch at rest, but lasting, long revenge." His resolutions to be himself tolerant often broke down, and he could not abide "men who pray" and such-like; but what could be expected from such a hero in such aworld! He had all the naïveté as well as the self-reliance of true greatness. He had no sooner become an undergraduate at Oxford than he printed a pamphlet on "The Necessity of Atheism," and sent copies to the Vice-Chancellor, the heads of houses, and all the bishops, with "a pretty letter in his own handwriting" to each. He was summoned before the University authorities, who "pleaded, implored, and threatened; on the other side, the unabashed and beardless boy maintaining his right to think, and declare his thoughts to others." Much evil as he believed of such vermin, he does not seem to have dreamed of the intolerance of which they were capable. Hogg—the dear and life-long friend who tried to seduce his wife—writes: "He rushed in; he was terribly agitated. 'I am expelled,' he said, as soon as he had recovered himself a little; 'I am expelled!'... He sat on the sofa, repeating with convulsive vehemence the words 'Expelled! expelled!'" Professor Dowden thinks "it was natural and perhaps expedient that measures should have been taken to vindicate the authority of the heads of the institution; ... but good feeling" would not have punished so severely what "was more an offence of the intellect than of the heart and will": for what was it "to fling out a boy's defiance against the first article of the Creed," compared with the drinking and disorderly life of some other undergraduates who were yet allowed to remain in the University? The conduct of the authorities was the less excusable that we have Mr. Hogg's authority for the fact that at this time "the purity and sanctity of his life were most conspicuous," and that "in no individual, perhaps, was the moral sense ever more completely developed than in Shelley." Of course, in face of such an authority as Mr. Hogg, the assertion of Thornton Hunt that "he was aware of facts which gave him to understand that Shelley while at college, in tampering with venal passions, had seriously injured his health; and that this was followed by a reaction 'marked by horror,'" is not to be listened to, and is therefore relegated to a footnote. Professor Dowden rightly thinks that Shelley might have been all the better had he left the University at the usual time, and with his mind weighted with more discipline and knowledge. "His voyage," says his biographer, "must needs have been fleet and far, and the craft, with fore and flying sails set, must often have run upon her side and drunk the water; all the more reason, therefore, for laying in some ballast below before she raced into the gale." Every one knows how the craft raced into the gale, with Miss Westbrook on board, as soon as the Oxford hawser was cut.Shelley might have done much worse. She was a good and attractive person. He began by liking her. "There are some hopes," he says, "of this dear little girl; she would be a divine little scion of infidelity if I could get hold of her." She seems to have been sincerely devoted to him and he afterwards to her, until circumstances unknown or undivulged made his home insupportable to her, and she became the "frantic idiot" who, though she would give Shelley money when she had it, was apparently not sufficiently "tolerant" upon other points—such as that of his proposition that she should enjoy the scenery of Switzerland in his company and that of her supplanter; and it certainly showed some narrowness of mind to cast herself, upon his final desertion of her, first into some desperation of living and afterwards into the Serpentine, when she might have shared, or at least witnessed, the "eternal rapture" and "divine aspirations" which her husband was enjoying in the arms of another woman. Poor little "idiot" as she was, she constitutes almost the only point in all this bewildering "romance of reality" upon which the mind can rest with any peace or pleasure.

What Shelley was at first he remained to the last: a beautiful, effeminate, arrogant boy—constitutionally indifferent to money, generous byimpulse, self-indulgent by habit, ignorant to the end of all that it most behoves a responsible being to know, and so conceited that his ignorance was incurable; showing at every turn the most infallible sign of a feeble intellect, a belief in human perfectibility; and rushing at once to the conclusion, when he or others met with suffering, that some one, not the sufferer, was doing grievous wrong. If to do what is right in one's own eyes is the whole of virtue, and to suffer for so doing is to be a martyr, then Shelley was the saint and martyr which a large number of—chiefly young—persons consider him to have been as a man; and if to have the faculty of saying everything in the most brilliant language and imagery, without having anything particular to say beyond sublime commonplaces and ethereal fallacies about love and liberty, is to be a "supreme" poet, then Shelley undoubtedly was such. But, as a man, Shelley was almost wholly devoid of the instincts of the "political animal," which Aristotle defines a man to be. If he could not see the reasons for any social institution or custom, he could not *feel* any; and forthwith set himself to convince the world that they were the invention of priests and tyrants. He was equally deficient in what is commonly understood by natural affection. The ties of relationship were no ties to him: for he could only *see* them as accidents. "I, like the God of the Jews," writes Shelley, "set up myself as no respecter of persons; and relationship is regarded by me as bearing that relation to reason which a band of straw does to fire." As these deficiencies were the cause of all the abnormal phenomena of his life, so they are at the root of, or rather are, the imperfections of his poetry, which is all splendour and sentiment and sensitiveness, and little or no true wisdom or true love. The very texture of his verse suffers from these causes. In his best poems it is firm, fluent, various, and melodious; but the more serious and subtle music of life which he had not in his heart he could not put into his rhythms; which no one who knows what rhythm is will venture to compare with the best of Tennyson's or Wordsworth's, far less with the best of our really "supreme" poets. A very great deal of his poetry is much like the soap-bubbles he was so fond of blowing—its superficies beauty, its substance wind; or like many a young lady who looks and moves and modulates her speech like a goddess, and chatters like an ape.

After Shelley, the chief male figure in this romance—which would be altogether incredible were it not real—is that of the guide, philosopher, and friend of the poet's youth, Godwin. Pecksniff is genteel comedy compared with the grim farce of this repulsive lover of wisdom as embodied in himself. Like the German poet who was entrusted by one friend to be the bearer of a sausage to another, and, bit by bit, ate it all on his way, Godwin "sincerely abhorred all that was sordid and mean; but he liked sausage"; and the way he combined the necessity for nibbling at Shelley's future fortune by making incessant claims, which the latter could only satisfy by repeated and ruinous post-obits, with the other necessity for keeping up the insulted and injured dignity of a man whom Shelley had wronged past pardon, is funny beyond description. His writing to tell Shelley that he had insulted him by giving him a heavy sum of money in the form of a cheque made payable to his (Godwin's) own name, thereby making the gift liable to be construed as such by the banker, and threatening solemnly not to receive the gift at all, unless the name was changed to "Hume" or any other the poet might select, is a touch which Shakespeare might have coveted for Ancient Pistol.

It appears that there still exists a good deal of writing by and concerning Shelley which it has not been deemed expedient to publish. A footnote, for instance, assures us that "a poetical epistle to Graham referring to his father in odious terms" is still "in existence"; and various other unprinted letters and poems are alluded to. But it is scarcely to be supposed that any future *Life of Shelley* will supersede Professor Dowden's—unless, indeed, it should be an abridgment, more suitable in bulk and perhaps in tone than the present publication is, for the use of those who, undazzled, or possibly repelled, by the glamour of Shelley's personality and revolutionary convictions, admire the meteoric splendour of his genius and allow it its not unimportant place in the permanent literature of England.

XV

BLAKE

BLAKE'S poetry, with the exception of four or five lovely lyrics and here and there in the other pieces a startling gleam of unquestionable genius, is mere drivel. A sensible person can easily distinguish between that which he cannot understand and that in which there is nothing to be understood. Mr. W. Rossetti, who is an enthusiast for "the much-maligned Paris Commune" and for Blake's poetry, says of some of the latter, where it is nearly at its worst, "We feel its potent and arcane influence, but cannot dismember this into articulated meanings." This sentence, if put into less exalted English, expresses tolerably well the aspect of mind with which we regard much of the writing of the Prophets and of the great ancient and modern mystics. Some light of their meaning forces itself through the, in most cases, purposely obscure cloud of their words and imagery; but when, by chance, a glimpse of the disk itself is caught, it is surprisingly strong, bright, and intelligible. Such writers are only spoken of with irreverence by those that would have given their verdict in favour of the famous Irishman who, being confronted with one witness swearing to having seen him take a handkerchief from another gentleman's pocket, brought four who testified with equal solemnity to not having seen him do any such thing. The obvious rule in regard to such writers is, "When you cannot understand a man's ignorance, think yourself ignorant of his understanding." Again, if a man's sayings are wholly unintelligible to us, he may claim the benefit of a small possibility of a doubt that his meanings may be too great and necessarily "arcane" for our powers of reception. But when a writer's works consist of a few passages of great beauty and such simplicity that a child may understand them—like Blake's "Chimney-Sweep," "Tiger," "Piping down the valleys wild," "Why was Cupid a boy?" and "Auguries of Innocence"—and a great deal more that is mere ill-expressed but perfectly intelligible platitude and commonplace mixed with petty spite, and a far larger quantity still which to the ear of the natural understanding is mere gibberish, he has no right to claim, as Blake does, that the latter shall be regarded as plenarily inspired, or, indeed, as being anything better than the delirious rubbish it obviously is.

Mr. W. Rossetti, though he goes a great way further in his admiration of Blake than reason can be shown for, does the cause of reason a good service in declaring his opinion that the poet was probably mad. "When," says he, "I find a man pouring forth conceptions and images for which he professes himself not responsible, and which are in themselves in the highest degree remote, nebulous, and intangible, and putting some of these, moreover, into words wherein congruent sequence and significance of expression or analogy are not to be traced, then I cannot resist a strong presumption that that man was in some true sense of the word mad." As Pope "could not take his tea without a stratagem," so Blake could not "mix his colours with diluted glue" without declaring that "the process was revealed to him by St. Joseph"; and it was the ghost of his brother who taught him the new, though, had we not been told otherwise, the not supernaturally wonderful device of saving the expense of ordinary typography by etching the words of his verses on the copper plate which bore their illustrations. Blake was morally as well as intellectually mad; proposing on one occasion, for example, that his wife should allow him to introduce a second partner to his bed, anddoing so with a *bonâ fide* unconsciousness of anything amiss in such a suggestion as perfect as that with which Shelley urged his wife to come and share the delights of a tour in Switzerland with him and his mistress Mary Godwin.

That "great wits to madness nearly are allied" is not true; but it is not only true but psychologically explicable that small "geniuses" often are so. Most children are geniuses before the dawn of moral and intellectual responsibilities; and there are some who remain, not children, but moral and intellectual manikins, all their lives. It must be confessed that conscience makes, not only cowards, but more or less dullards, of us all. The child, that

Mighty prophet, seer blest,
On whom those truths do rest
Which we are toiling all our lives to find,

owes his power of vision to his not being able to see the flaming sword of conscience which turns every way, and hinders all men but a very few from getting a glimpse through the closed gates of Paradise. Yet it is better to be a purblind man with a conscience than a seeing manikin with none. It is better still, and best of all, when the man of developed intellect and fully accepted responsibilities retains a cherished memory of and an innocent sympathy with the knowledge that cameto him in childhood and early youth, and uses his trained powers of expression in order to make the world partakers of those thoughts and feelings which had no tongue when they first arose in him, and leave no memory in the mass of men until the man of true and sane genius touches chords of recollection that would otherwise have slept in them for ever. One of the few really good things ever said by Hazlitt is that "men of genius spend their lives in teaching the world what they themselves learned before they were twenty."

For the time, however, the manikin type of genius is all the fashion, especially with a class of critics who have it in their power to give notoriety, if they cannot give fame. Craziness alone passes at present for a strong presumption of genius, and where genius is really found in company therewith it is at once pronounced "supreme." This is partly because most people can see that craziness has something abnormal about it, and are ready, therefore, to identify it with genius, of which most persons only know that it also is "abnormal"; and partly because the manikin mind is always red republican, and ardent in its hatred of kings, priests, "conventions," the "monopoly" of property and of women, and all other hindrances put in the way of virtue, liberty, and happiness by the wicked "civilizee."

Blake, as an artist, is a more important figure than Blake the poet; and naturally so, for the smallest good poem involves a consecutiveness and complexity of thought which are only required in paintings of a character which Blake rarely attempted. Yet, even as a painter his reputation has until lately been much exaggerated. The recent exhibition of his collected drawings and paintings was a great blow to the fame which had grown up from a haphazard acquaintance by his admirers with a few sketches or an illustrated poem. Here and there there was a gleam of such pure and simple genius as is often revealed in the speech of a finely natured child amid its ordinary chatter; here and there the expression of a tender or distempered dream, which was not like anything else in the spectator's experience; now and then an outline that had a look of Michael Angelo, with sometimes hints which might have formed the themes of great works, and which justified the saying of Fuseli that "Blake is damned good to steal from"; but the effect of the whole collection was dejecting and unimpressive, and did little towards confirming its creator's opinion that Titian, Reynolds, and Gainsborough were bad artists, and Blake, Barry, and Fuseli good ones.

XVI

ROSSETTI AS A POET

THE claims of Rossetti as a painter and a poet have obtained a full and generous recognition; and he has acquired a standing in either art which will in all probability abide, though it is far too soon to attempt any estimate of his relative position in the permanent ranks of artists and writers. His thoughtfulness, and the clearness and intensity of his perceptions, do not require to be insisted upon, nor the almost unexampled way in which he has merged—and often, it must be admitted, confounded—the functions of painter and poet. This he has done to the detriment of his perfection in either art; in neither of which can he be truly said to have attained the character of mastery which may be found, more or less, in almost all other workers of equal genius with himself, and sometimes in those whose natural qualifications have been inferior to his. Littleof his drawing and none of his painting can be enjoyed without the drawback of some sense of manifest technical failure; and nearly all his poetry—which is more or less difficult by reason of the quick succession of out-of-the-way thoughts and images, needing the closest attention for their appreciation—is rendered unnecessarily so by language which rarely has the fluency of perfection. In the two or three instances in which his verse becomes fluent and more or less masterly—notably in the "Burden of Nineveh" and "Jenny"—it ceases to be characteristic or subtle. The "Burden of Nineveh" might have been written by Southey, or any other writer of forcible words and thoughts in somewhat commonplace rhythm. This fact, that fluency fails him as soon as he gets upon his own proper ground, renders it extremely difficult to discern and to describe exactly what that ground is. Style, which is the true expression of the poet's individuality—the mark by which we discover, not what, but how, he thinks and feels—is almost suffocated, in Rossetti's most characteristic work, by voluntary oddities of manner and by a manifest difficulty in so moving in the bonds of verse as to convert them into graces. If subtle thoughts and vivid imagery were all that went to make a poet, Rossetti would stand very high. But these qualities must havethe running commentary and musical accompaniment of free feeling, which only a correspondingly subtle and vivid versification can express, before they can be allowed to constitute a claim to the highest poetical rank. Rossetti as a versifier was as technically defective as Rossetti as a painter; his best poems and his best paintings are the outcome, not only of very high aims—which are as common as blackberries—but of very high aims deeply and characteristically felt; and his superiority to many far more technically perfect artists results from the fact that his characteristic feeling is strong enough to make itself powerfully, however indistinctly, perceived through the mist and obstructions of his mannerism and defective verse.

Like all men of strong artistic individuality combined with serious artistic faults, Rossetti has had a great influence upon the literature of his day—such an influence as comparatively faultless writers never exert, at least in their time. Many young versifiers and painters fancy they are reproducing Rossetti's intensity when they are only imitating the most prevailing fault of his art, its tensity. His brother, William Rossetti, in his modest and judicious introduction to these volumes, tells how he and Gabriel used to amuse themselves in making *bouts-rimés*. William saysof his brother's literary toys of this sort: "Some have a *faux air* of intensity of meaning, as well as of expression; but their real core of significance is small." It cannot be denied that a careful scrutiny of much of Rossetti's published work is open to this criticism. It is tense without being intense. This fault is his great attraction to his imitators, whose every sensation is represented as a pang, delicious or otherwise, and whose mental sky is a canopy of iron destiny compared with which the melancholy of Byron, which likewise had so many copyists, was no more than a pleasant shade.

In endeavouring to do justice to Rossetti it must be remembered that, though born and bred in England, he was an Italian by blood and sympathy. His acquaintance with Englishmen and English books was by no means wide. Love, the constant theme of his art, is in some of his most important poems, not the English love whose stream is steady affection and only its occasional eddies passion, and which, when disappointed, does not cease to be love, though it becomes sorrow: but the Italian ardour, in perennial crisis, which stabs its rival and hates its object, if she refuses its satisfaction, as ardently as it worships her so long as there is hope. The limitations, also, which characterise Rossetti's poetry belongto Italian poetry itself. There is little breadth in it, but much acuteness. Dante is to Shakespeare as the Peak of Teneriffe to the tableland of Tibet; and, as any reader of Rossetti's translations of the minor Italian poets may see, the same proportion prevails between them and the lesser singers of England. It is therefore quite unfair to try an essentially Italian poet, like Rossetti, by comparing his works with the classical poetry of a nation which, for combined breadth and height, far surpasses the poetry of all other languages present and past, with the doubtful exception of the Greek. The English language itself is not made for Italian thought and passion. It has about four times as many vowel sounds as Italian and a corresponding consonantal power; that is to say, it differs from the Italian about as much as an organ differs from a flute. Rossetti uses little beside the flute-notes of our English organ; and, if he had made himself complete master of those notes, it would have been the most that could have been expected of him. In appearance and manners Rossetti was thoroughly Italian. In his youth especially he had the sweet and easy courtesy peculiar to his nation. His brother says, "There was a certain British bluffness streaking the finely poised Italian suppleness and facility." This describes, better than perhaps Mr. William Rossetti intended, a characteristic which occasionally, but fortunately not often, appears in his poetry, which is most pleasing when it is least "streaked" with British bluffness: as it is, for example, in "Jenny."

Rossetti's power is chiefly shown in his long ballads, such as "Sister Helen," "The Bride's Prelude," "Rose Mary," and "The King's Tragedy." Had these been found in Percy's "Relics," they would have constituted the chief ornaments of that collection. As it is, it is impossible not to feel that they are more or less anachronisms, both in spirit and in form. The repetition of a refrain through the fifty stanzas or so of "Sister Helen," the most forcible of all these lyrical narratives, has no sufficient justification for its interruption of the fiercely flowing history. A refrain which extends to more than three or four stanzas requires and originally assumed a musical accompaniment. The constant high-pressure of passion in these ballads is also an anachronism; and to the cultured modern reader this character is calculated to defeat the poet's purpose, giving him an impression of cold instead of warmth, as if the fire had a salamander instead of a heart in its centre. A kindred fault, which Rossetti has in common with some of the most famous poets of the century, is that of conferring upon all his images an acute and independent clearness which is never found in the natural and truly poetical expression of feeling. It is true, and great poets (especially Shakespeare) have noted it, that in extreme crises of passion there will sometimes be a moment of calm in which the minutiæ of some most trifling object or circumstance will, as it were, photograph themselves upon the mind. But this præternatural calm is only the "eye of the storm"; and to scatter broadcast, over a long poem, imagery with the sharpest outlines is to prove, not only that it has not been written from true passion, but that the poet has not even observed the phenomena of true passion. Such independent force and clearness of imagery can only be justified in poems of the very lowest type of artistic construction, such as Schiller's "Song of the Bell" and "Childe Harold," which scarcely profess to have more unity than is to be found in a scrap-book. A fine poem may or may not be full of "fine things"; but, if it does abound in them, their independent value should only appear when they are separated from their context. In Rossetti, as in several other modern poets of great reputation, we are constantly being pulled up, in the professedly fiery course of a tale of passion, to observe the moss on a rock or the note of a chaffinch. High finish has nothing to do with this quality of extreme definiteness in detail; indeed, it is more often exercised by the perfect poet in blurring outlines than in giving them acuteness. It must be admitted, however, that Rossetti had an unusual temptation to this kind of excess in his extraordinary faculty for seeing objects in such a fierce light of imagination as very few poets have been able to throw upon external things. He can be forgiven for spoiling a tender lyric by a stanza such as this, which seems scratched with an adamantine pen upon a slab of agate—

But the sea stands spread
As one wall with the flat skies,
Where the lean black craft, like flies,
Seem wellnigh stagnated,
Soon to drop off dead.

Though the foregoing strictures apply to a large portion of Rossetti's work, there is a really precious residuum which they do not touch. There are several pieces—such as "Love's Nocturn," "The Portrait," "A Little While," and many sonnets—which are full of natural feeling expressed with simple and subtle art; and in much of his work there is a rich and obscure glow of insight into depths too profound and too sacred for clearspeech, even if they could be spoken: a sort of insight not at all uncommon in the great art of past times, but exceedingly rare in the art of our own.

XVII

MR. SWINBURNE'S SELECTIONS

IT has probably been a misfortune for Mr. Swinburne's growth as a poet that no winter of critical neglect preceded the full recognition of his very remarkable talents. His best friends must allow that he is still somewhat younger in judgment than in his years and experience of authorship. It is not, however, much to be wondered at that he should have been tempted to rest content with having apparently attained at a single step a height of reputation to reach which has been with most poets the work of hard climbing during many years. Mr. Swinburne is still in the prime of life and in full possession of his powers, and some of his later work shows that he has that continued power of growth which is one of the greatest privileges of genius. If he will only listen to his own critical conscience, he may yet do work better and much more enduring than any he has yet done. He cannot, indeed, hope to excel certain single passages of prose and verse in which he has attained a character of breadth and poetic ardour scarcely to be found in any other writer of the time; but he can (and there have of late been signs that he intends to) modify his manner of thinking and writing so that his best—which is very good indeed—may not be discredited by so much of the jejune in thought and composition as is to be found in a great deal of his work heretofore. Hitherto Mr. Swinburne has been too much given to protesting; which is not the poet's work, even when it is done wisely. In his future writing we shall probably hear more of the whisper of affirmative wisdom than the whirlwind of passionate negation; he will recognise more and more fully that the world is not and never will be made up of Swinburnes and Rossettis, and that it is vain to denounce popular beliefs and institutions, when he has only, to set up in their places, others which are, and for ever will be, unintelligible by the great majority of mankind, and inapplicable to their demands. The people will always insist on having kings and priests; and Mr. Swinburne has, no doubt, had his eyes too well opened by very recent history not to discern that it would be of little use to dethrone King Log in favour of Prime Minister Stork, or to unfrock an Archbishop of Canterbury in order to transfer his authority to a General Booth.

Hitherto it has been impossible not to feel that there has been some disproportion between Mr. Swinburne's power of saying things and the things he has to say. This defect of the "body of thought," which Coleridge once complained was wanting in an otherwise good poem, has reacted upon Mr. Swinburne's language itself, producing sometimes a reiteration of words and imagery surpassing even that which is to be found in the works of Shelley, and which in them arose from the same inadequacy of matter. For example, in a passage of thirteen lines in the present volume we have "flowery forefront of the year," "foam-flowered strand," "blossom-fringe," "flower-soft face," and "spray-flowers"; and in Mr. Swinburne's poems generally it must be confessed that flowers, stars, waves, flames and three or four other entities of the natural order, come in so often as to suggest some narrowness of observation and vocabulary. This defect, also, is less manifest than it used to be, though probably the abandonment to the mere joy of words, which is natural and not altogether ungraceful in a writer who can use them so splendidly, will always be a characteristic of Mr. Swinburne's poetry. It reminds us of the rapture of Tristram in the truly magnificentdescription of the bath he took before breakfast in "Sea and Sunrise," and the reader is often carried with like joy upon the waves of words without troubling himself as to whether he and the poet are not both out of their depth.

Mr. Swinburne's mode of dealing with human passions is somewhat of an anachronism. His heroes and heroines, like those of the old English drama and the Scandinavian poems, often become heroic by the sacrifice of humanity, and, thereby, of the reader's sympathy. The pictures of Mary Queen of Scots and of Iseult in this volume, for instance, though painted with a great brush are not truly great, because they are not greatly true—at all events, to any conditions which the modern world recognises or should desire to recognise. Nor, granting that the characters and situations are poetical, is the execution quite what it ought to be. The effects are obtained by a cumulative rather than a developing process; and, at the end of a long poem or passage full of strong words and images, the idea of strength thence derived is rather that given by a hill than the living hole of a huge tree.

Mr. Swinburne's metrical practice should be criticised with respect; for he has an unquestionably fine ear, and has ransacked the literature of all times in order to discover and appropriate, ormodify to his own uses, a number of movements which, unlike our familiar English metres, are whirlwinds and blasts of passion in themselves. Such metres, however, should be sparingly used. They almost satisfy the ear without any accompaniment of sound meaning, and evoke, as it were by a trick, a current of emotion that is independent of any human feeling in the poet himself. This is a great temptation, and Mr. Swinburne has not always avoided the traps which he has thus set for himself. Such metres have, moreover, the disadvantage of fixing in too peremptory a manner the key in which the poems written in them must be sustained. They allow none of the endless modulations which are open to the poet who writes in almost any of our native and less emphatic measures. Mr. Swinburne has the less reason for resorting so habitually as he does to this too easy means of obtaining passionate effect, inasmuch as some of his very best and most effective passages are written in our common metres. Witness the almost incomparable apostrophe to Athens, in "Erechtheus" (unfortunately not included in these selections), and "Sea and Sunrise," and "Herse."

There is one still easier and far less excusable source of effect which every friend of the poet must rejoice to see that he has of late abandoned. There is nothing in the *Selections* which a schoolgirl might not be permitted to read and understand, if she could; and there are a number of pieces about children which are so full of pure and tender perceptions as to cause a doubt whether, in some of his earlier writings, the poet was not wantonly flouting the world's opinion rather than expressing any very real phase of his own feeling.

XVIII

ARTHUR HUGH CLOUGH

CLOUGH worshipped Truth with more than the passion of a lover, and his writings are, for the most part, the tragic records of a life-long devotion to a mistress who steadily refused his embraces; but as it is greatly better to have loved without attaining than to have attained without loving, so Clough's ardent and unrewarded stumblings in the dark towards his adored though unseen divinity are greatly more attractive and edifying to those who have shared, successfully or not, the same passion, than is that complacent fruition of her smiles which she often accords to those who are contented to be no more than her speaking acquaintances. Regarded from a purely intellectual point of view, Clough's utterances on religion, duty, etc., are little better than the commonplaces which in these days pass through the mind and more or less affect the feelings of almost every intelligent and educated youth before he is twenty years of age; but there are commonplaces which cease to be such, and become indefinitely interesting, in proportion as they are animated by moral ardour and passion. Speech may work good by warming as well as by enlightening; and if Clough's writings teach no new truth, they may inflame the love of truth, which is perhaps as great a service. Though he professes that he can nowhere see light where light is most necessary and longed for, his mind is utterly opposed to the negative type; and he exactly exemplifies the class of believer whom Richard Hooker endeavours to comfort, in his great sermon on "the perpetuity of faith in the elect," by the reminder that a longing to believe is implicit faith, and that we cannot sorrow for the lack of that which we interiorly hold to be nonexistent. A question that must suggest itself to most readers is, What is the use and justification of these endless and tautological lamentations over the fact—as Clough conceived it to be—that, for such as him at least, "Christ is not risen"? The reply is, that the responsibility of the publication of so much that is profoundly passionate but far from profoundly intellectual scepticism was not his. With the exception of some not very significant critical essays, his prose consists of letters, which were of course not meant for the public; and the greater part of his poetry remained to the day of Clough's death in his desk, and would probably never have left it, with his consent, unless to be put in the fire.

Those who recognise in the "Bothie" Clough's almost solitary claim to literary eminence must somewhat wonder at the considerable figure he stands for in the estimation of the present generation. The fact is that Clough, like James Spedding, was personally far more impressive than his works; and the singularly strong effect produced among his friends by the extreme simplicity and shy kindliness of his life and manners, and the at once repellent and alluring severity of his truthfulness, gave his character a consequence beyond that of his writings with all who knew him though ever so slightly; and the halo of this sanctity hangs, through the report of his friends, about all that he has done, and renders cold criticism of it almost impossible. No one who knew Clough can so separate his personality from his writings as to be able to criticise them fairly as literature; no one who has not known him can understand their value as the outcome of character.

The impressionable and feminine element, which is manifest in all genius, but which in truly effectivegenius is always subordinate to power of intellect, had in Clough's mind the preponderance. The masculine power of intellect consists scarcely so much in the ability to see truth, as in the tenacity of spirit which cleaves to and assimilates the truth when it is found, and which steadfastly refuses to be blown about by every wind of doctrine and feeling. The reiterated theme of Clough's poetry is that the only way of forgetting certain problems now, and of securing their solution hereafter, is to do faithfully our nearest duty. This is no new teaching: it is that of every religion and all philosophy. But Clough had no power of trusting patiently to the promise, "Do my commandments, and you shall know of the doctrine." This was the ruin of what might otherwise have been a fine poetic faculty. A "Problem" will not sing even in the process of solution, much less while it is only a hopeless and irritating "Pons." Clough was curiously attracted by Emerson, of whom he spoke as the only great contemporary American. Now Emerson, at his very best, never approached greatness. He was at highest only a brilliant metaphysical epigrammatist. But a religion without a dogma, and with only one commandment, "Thou shalt neither think nor do anything that is customary," had great attractions for Clough; to whom it never seems to have occurred that thevast mass of mankind, for whose moral and religious welfare he felt so keenly, has not and never can have a religion of speechless aspirations and incommunicable feelings, and that to teach men to despise custom is to cut the immense majority of them adrift from all moral restraint. The promise that we shall all be priests and kings seems scarcely to be for this world. At all events we are as far from its fulfilment now as we were two thousand years ago; and we shall not be brought nearer to it by any such outpourings of sarcastic discontent as go to the making of such poems as the tedious Mephistophelian drama called "Dipsychus," which Clough had the good sense not to publish, though it is included with many others of equally doubtful value in posthumous editions of his works. This class of his poems possesses, indeed, a lively interest for a great many people of our own time, who are in the painful state of moral and religious ferment which these verses represent; but it is a mere accident of the time that there is any considerable audience for such utterances, and in a generation or two it is probable that most men will feel surprise that there could ever have been a public who found poetry in this sort of matter.

The "Bothie of Tober-na-Vuolich" is the only considerable poem of Clough's in which he seems, for a time, to have got out of his slough of introspection and doubt and to have breathed the healthy air of nature and common humanity. In spite of many artistic shortcomings, this poem is so healthy, human, and original, that it can scarcely fail to survive when a good deal of far more fashionable verse shall have disappeared from men's memories. The one infallible note of a true poet—the power of expressing himself in rhythmical movements of subtilty and sweetness which baffle analysis—is also distinctly manifest in passages of the "Bothie," passages the music of which was, we fancy, lingering in the ear of Tennyson when he wrote certain parts of "Maud." The originality of this idyl is beyond question. It is not in the least like any other poem, and an occasionally ostentatious touch of the manner of "Herman and Dorothea" seems to render this originality all the more conspicuous in the main. Another note of poetical power, scarcely less questionable than is that of sweetness and subtilty of rhythm, is the warm and pure breath of womanhood which is exhaled from the love-passages of this poem. Clough seems to have felt, in the presence of a simple and amiable woman, a mystery of life which acted for a time as the rebuke and speechless solution of all doubts and intellectual distresses. These passages in the "Bothie," and, in a less degree, some others in the "Amours de Voyage," stand, in the disturbed course of Clough's ordinary verse, like the deep, pure, and sky-reflecting pools which occasionally appear in the course of a restless mountain river.

XIX

EMERSON

THE life and writings of Emerson owe their chief claim on our attention to the fact that they represent with singular force a line of thought and belief—if belief it can be called—which an immense number of the young, intelligent, and sincere of the past and present generation have been endeavouring to follow, though as yet without any remarkable or satisfactory results. "Every man is potentially a man of genius," is the one dogma of Emerson's religion—though it is nowhere put thus plainly by him; and its one commandment is "Be a man of genius." Absolute nonconformity with everything, we are taught, is the first condition of personal and social well-being; and we are enjoined to look upon our individual insight as our one infallible guide, though it may bid us go one way to-day and the opposite to-morrow. At the time when Emerson was debating with himself as to whether he should throw up his office as Unitarian preacher he seems to have had some searchings of heart as to the validity of the new doctrine. "How," he writes, in his Journal, "shall the droning world get on if all its *beaux esprits* recalcitrate upon its approved forms and accepted constitutions and quit them in order to be single-minded? The double-refiners would produce at the other end the double-damned." This is perhaps the wisest thing ever said by Emerson; but he nevertheless chose his part definitively with the "double refiners." "I hate preaching," he writes in a subsequent page of his Journal. "Preaching is a pledge, and I wish to say what I feel and think to-day, with the proviso that to-morrow perhaps I shall contradict it all." In the free use of his proviso he accordingly, for the remainder of his life, followed and taught others to follow what he called "intuition," even though it should not wait for "to-morrow" to contradict itself. For example, in the last page but one of the essay on "Character" we are instructed to reject the doctrine of the divinity of Christ because "the mind requires a victory to the senses, a force of character which will convert judge, jury, soldier, and king and on the following page we are told that, "when that love which is all-suffering, all-abstaining, all-aspiring ... comes into our streets and houses, only the pure and aspiring can know its face."

Emerson's life, journals, and letters considerably modify the impression which his published essays and lectures are calculated to leave—namely, that he was a mere stringer-together of lively thoughts, images, and poetical epigrams. He seems to have made the best of his own humanity, and to have always done the right according to his judgment, though the doing of it sometimes involved serious pecuniary inconvenience, and, as in the case of his opposition to the fugitive slave law, violent popular disapprobation. He was kindly and moral in his family and social relationships, and was conscientious even to a fault in avoiding those venial sins of language to which the most of us are perhaps too indifferent. His American admirers sometimes spoke of him as an "angel." At any rate, he was a sort of sylph. He noted of his compatriots generally that "they have no passions, only appetites." He seems to have had neither passion nor appetite; and there was an utter absence of "nonsense" about him which made it almost impossible to be intimate with him. Margaret Fuller, his closest friend, and even his wife, whom he loved in his own serene way, seem to have chafed under the impossibility of getting within the adamantine sphere of self-consciousnesswhich surrounded him. He not only could not forget himself, but he could not forget his grammar; and when he talked he seemed rather to be "composing" his thoughts than thinking them. His friend and admirer, Mr. Henry James the elder, complains that for this reason his conversation was without charm. "For nothing ever came but epigrams, sometimes clever, sometimes not." His manners and discourse were, however, invariably kind and amiable. He never seems to have uttered a personal sarcasm, and only once in his life to have been seriously angry. This was on occasion of the famous fugitive slave law, which he indignantly declared would be disobeyed, if need be, by himself and every honest man.

Dr. W. H. Furness writes of Emerson: "We were babies and schoolfellows together. I don't think he ever engaged in boys' plays.... I can as little remember when he was not literary in his pursuits as when I first made his acquaintance." Indeed, "orating" was in Emerson's blood. Nearly all his known ancestors and relatives seem to have been "ministers" of some denomination or other. His school-days—though he never became a scholar in any department of learning—began before he was three years old. His father complains of the baby of two years and odd months— "Ralph does not read very well yet"; and duringall the rest of his youth Dr. Furness says that he grew up under "the pressure of I know not how many literary atmospheres." Add to this the fact that his father and mother and his aunt—who was the chief guide of his nonage—were persons who seemed to think that love could only be manifested by severe duty, and rarely showed him any signs of the weaknesses of "affection," and we have as bad a bringing-up for a moral, philosophical, and religious teacher as could well have been devised. "The natural first, and afterwards the spiritual." Where innocent joy and personal affection have not been main factors of early experience the whole life wants the key to Christianity; and a rejection of all faith—except that in "genius," "over-soul," "a somewhat which makes for righteousness," or some other such impotent abstraction—is, in our day, almost inevitable in a mind of constitutional sincerity like Emerson's, especially when such sincerity is unaccompanied, as it was in him, by a warm and passionate nature and its intellectual correlative, a vigorous conscience. Emerson, though a good man—that is, one who lived up to his lights—had little or no conscience. He admired good, but did not love it; he denounced evil, but did not hate it, and did not even maintain that it was hateful, but only greatly inexpedient.

Though Emerson could not see that a religion of which there is nothing left but an "over-soul" is much the same thing as a man of whom there is nothing left but his hat, the religious bodies to which he was for many years more or less attached were less devoid of humour, and the joke of a faith without a dogma became, in time, too much for their seriousness. Consequently they agreed amicably to part, and Emerson pursued his course; that which had hitherto been called "preaching" becoming thenceforward lecturing and "orating."

There can be no greater misfortune for a sincere and truthful mind like Emerson's than to have to get a living by "orating." This was his predicament, however; and there can be no doubt that his mind and his writings were the worse for this necessity. His philosophy afforded him only a very narrow range of subject. In all his essays and lectures he is but ringing the changes upon three or four ideas—which are really commonplace, though his sprightly wit and imagination give them freshness; and it is impossible to read any single essay, much less several in succession, without feeling that the licence of tautology is used to its extremest limits. In a few essays—for example, "The Poet," "Character," and "Love"—the writer's heart is so much in the matter that these endless variations of one idea have the effect of music which delights us to the end with the reiteration of an exceedingly simple theme; but in many other pieces it is impossible not to detect that weariness of the task of having to coin dollars out of transcendental sentiments to which Emerson's letters and journals often bear witness. But, whether delighted with or weary of his labour, there is no progress in his thought, which resembles the spinning of a cockchafer on a pin rather than the flight of a bird on its way from one continent to another.

Emerson's was a sweet and uniformly sunny spirit; but the sunshine was that of the long Polar day, which enlightens but does not fructify. It never even melted the icy barrier which separated his soul from others; and men and women were nothing to him, because he never got near enough to understand them. Hence his journals and letters about his visits to Europe, and especially to England, are curiously superficial in observation. He made many acute and witty remarks, such as, "Every Englishman is a House of

Commons, and expects that you will not end your speech without proposing a measure;" but, on the whole, he quite misunderstood the better class of our countrymen, of whom, in his second visit to England, he had the opportunity of seeing a good deal. Although there was much constitutionalreserve, there was no real reticence in him. His ethereal, unimpassioned ideas had, indeed, nothing in them that, for him, commanded reticence; and he concluded that the best sort of Englishmen were without any motives that "transcend" sense, because he did not feel, as all such Englishmen do, that though that which transcends sense may be infinitely dearer than all else, and even because it is so dear, it is better not to talk of things which can scarcely be spoken of without inadequacy and even an approach to nonsense. Many an Englishman would turn aside with a jest from any attempt to lead him into "transcendental" talk, not because he was less, but because he was more "serious" than his interlocutor; and also because the very recognition of certain kinds of knowledge involves the recognition of obligations, to confess directly or indirectly the fulfilment or neglect of which implies either self-praise or self-blame, which, in ordinary circumstances, are alike indecent. In fact, Emerson was totally deficient in the religious sense, which is very strong in the hearts of a vast number of Englishmen who own to no fixed creed, but who would be revolted by the profound and unconscious irreverence with which Emerson was in the habit of speaking and writing of the most sacred things and names. The name of "Jesus" frequently occurs in such sentences as this: "NorJesus, nor Pericles, nor Cæsar, nor Angelo, nor Washington," etc.

If we put aside Emerson's unconscious malpractices in this sort, the attitude of his mind with regard to the serious beliefs of the world were too childish for resentment or exposure. It is as if one should be angry with a young lady who should simper, "Oh, my religion is the religion of the Sermon on the Mount!" in answer to an attempt to talk with her about Bossuet or Hooker.

XX

CRABBE AND SHELLEY

THE firmament of fame is full of variable stars, and they are nowhere thicker than in that great constellation of poets which marks the end of the last and the commencement of this century. Among the names of Byron, Moore, Rogers, Southey, Wordsworth, Coleridge, Keats, Shelley, Burns, Campbell, Crabbe, Cowper, and Scott, there are only two the lustre of whose names has remained perfectly steady and seems likely to remain so. Two or three, which blazed forth at once as luminaries of the first magnitude, have gradually and persistently waned—whether or not ever to recover any part of their lost splendour is very doubtful. The light of one or two others has fluctuated violently, and continues to do so, with a manifest diminution, however, in their total sum of light; one or two others have suffered a distinct degradation from first into second or third class lustres, and atpresent show no sign of further alteration. Two at least have grown astonishingly in conspicuousness, and now glow like the Dog-star and Aldebaran—though there are not wanting sky-critics who declare that they discern conditions of coming change and retrogression; and one at least has almost disappeared from the heaven of public recognition, not, however, without prognostications from some of an assured reassertion of a moderate if not predominating position.

To quit figures of speech, Coleridge and Burns—though poets of very different calibre—are the only two of the thirteen above mentioned whose reputations have been altogether unaffected by the violent changes of literary fashion which have taken place in the course of the century. Each of these two poets has written a good deal which the world will willingly let die; but Coleridge in his great way, and Burns in his comparatively small way, have done a certain moderate amount of work so thoroughly and manifestly well that no sane critic has ever called it into question or ever will. By the leaders of poetic fashion Moore and Rogers have come to be accounted as almost nowhere as poets. Southey and Cowper now depend mainly for their fame upon a few small pieces, which in their own day were not regarded as of much account in comparison with such works as *The Task* and *The Curse of Kehama*; Campbell now lives only, but vigorously, in a few lyrics. Who but Mr. Ruskin is there that would not laugh now to hear the name of Scott coupled with those of Keats and Shelley? Byron, who once outblazed all others, is now considered, by many judges not altogether to be disregarded, less as a great fixed star than as a meteor formed from earthly fumes condensed and for a time incandescent in the upper air. Wordsworth's fame, though all agree that it is assured, has suffered and is likely still to suffer some fluctuations; and, when poetry is talked about in circles of modern experts, no one ever hears of Crabbe, though here and there one comes upon some literary oddity who maintains that he has as good a claim as Shelley to a place in the heavens of abiding fame. As this, to most modern ears astounding, paradox is certainly maintained, in private at least, by several persons whose opinion the most advanced critic would not think of despising, it may be worth while to see what can be said for it.

Things, it is said, are best known by comparison with their opposites; and, if so, surely Crabbe must be best illustrated by Shelley and Shelley by Crabbe. Shelley was an atheist and profoundly immoral; but his irreligion was radiant with pious imagination, and his immorality delicately and strictly conscientious. Crabbe was a most sincereChristian in faith and life; but his religion and morality were intolerant, narrow, and scrupulous, and sadly wanting in all the modern graces. Shelley had no natural feeling or affection and the greatest sensitiveness; Crabbe had the tenderest and strongest affections, but his nerves and æsthetic constitution were of the coarsest. Shelley's taste often stood him in the stead of morality. He would have starved rather than write begging letters to Thurlow, Burke, and other magnates, as Crabbe did when he wanted to better his condition as an apothecary's apprentice. Crabbe's integrity produced some of the best effects of taste, and made him at once an equal in manners with the dukes and statesmen with whom he associated as soon as he had been taken from his beggary by Burke. Through years and years of poverty and almost hopeless trial Crabbe was a devoted and faithful lover, and afterwards as devoted and faithful a husband to his "Myra," whom he adored in verses that justified some one's description of his style as "Pope in worsted stockings." Shelley breathes eternal vows in music of the spheres, to woman after woman, whom he will abandon and speak or write of with hatred and contempt as soon as their persons have ceased to please him. Crabbe knew nothing of the "ideal," but loved all actualities, especially unpleasant ones, upon which he wouldturn the electric light of his peculiar powers of perception till the sludge and dead dogs of a tidal river shone. Jeffrey described the true position of Crabbe among poets better than any one else has done when he wrote, "He has represented his villagers and humble burghers as altogether as dissipated and more dishonest and discontented than the profligates of higher life.... He may be considered as the satirist of low life—an occupation sufficiently arduous, and in a great degree new and original in our language." In this his proper vocation Crabbe is so far from being a "Pope in worsted stockings," that his lines often resemble the strokes of Dryden's sledge-hammer rather than the stings of his successor's cane. But, when uninspired by the intensely disagreeable or vicious, Crabbe's "diction" is to modern ears, for the most part, intolerable. In his cooler moments he poured forth thousands of such couplets as

It seems to us that our Reformers knew
Th' important work they undertook to do.

And to such vile newspaper prose he not only added the ghastly adornment of verse, but also frequently enlivened it with the "poetic licences" and Parnassian "lingo" of the Pope period. What a contrast with Shelley! He erred quite as much as Crabbe did from the imaginative realitywhich is the true ideal; but it was all in the opposite way. If Crabbe's eye, in its love for the actual and concrete, dwelt too habitually upon the hardness and ugliness of the earth on which he trod, Shelley's thoughts and perceptions were for the most part

Pinnacled dim in the intense inane

of a fancy which had no foundation in earth or heaven. His poetry has, however, the immortal reality of music; and his songs *are* songs, though they may be often called "songs without words," the words meaning so little though they sound so sweet.

    This "parallel"—as lines starting and continued in opposite directions have got to be called—might be carried much further with advantage to the student of poetry; and the comparison might be still more profitable if the best poems of Coleridge were examined as illustrations of the true poetic reality from which Crabbe and Shelley diverge equally, but in contrary ways. Crabbe mistakes actuality for reality; Shelley's imagination is unreal. Coleridge, when he is himself, whether he is in the region of actuality, as in "Genevieve," or in that of imagination, as in "Christabel," is always both real and ideal in the only true poetic sense, in which reality and ideality are truly one.In each of these poems, as in every work of true art, there is a living idea which expresses itself in every part, while the complete work remains its briefest possible expression, so that it is as absurd to ask What is its idea? as it would be to ask what is the idea of a man or of an oak. This idea cannot be a simple negation; and simple evil—which is so often Crabbe's theme—is simple negation. On the other hand, good, in order to be the ground of the ideal in art, must be intelligible—that is to say, imaginatively credible, though it may want the conditions of present actuality. But is there any such ideal as this in Shelley?

XXI

SHALL SMITH HAVE A STATUE?

THE modern practice of sending the hat round for money to set up in the Abbey or elsewhere a statue, or at least a bust, of Smith, during or immediately after his lifetime, in grateful remembrance of the service or pleasure he may have done us, can rarely be indulged without danger of making him and ourselves ridiculous in the eyes of our children; or even in our own, should we survive for a few years the amiable folly of having raised an abiding memorial of our possibly transient enthusiasm. There could have been no doubt of the propriety of setting up a statue to the Duke of Wellington after Waterloo, however much there may reasonably have been about the propriety of the statue itself which the ladies of England dedicated to the hero. But even in the case of such obvious and measurable merits as those of warriors, it is best not to be in a hurry. Historicalcriticism has discovered that the credit of great battles and even campaigns has not always been rightly due to the commanders-in-chief. Again, improvements like those of the steam jet, by which it became at once possible to raise the rate of railway travelling from under ten to over fifty miles an hour, the penny post, and the electric telegraph, are certainly matters for permanent memorials, provided that they are raised to the right men. But improvements and inventions of this magnitude scarcely ever are, in the first instance, attributed to the right men, who are generally more or less obscure and unrewarded geniuses. It is the practical man, who has the quickness to see the money value of a great invention and the means of removing the last external hindrance to its popular use, that gets the statue, and the money too. Few would envy him the latter; but it is cruel to him no less than to ourselves to be in such haste to decorate him with a laurel crown, which the touch of time may change into a fool's cap. Again, unless statues are due to good intentions ardently prosecuted without reference to results, we ought to be very careful how we impose immortality upon great philanthropists and humanitarians. It would not have been for the abiding happiness and honour of the two eminent prelates and the able editor who lately constituted themselves highcommissioners of public morality, to have had their images set up in Hyde Park back to back, like the figure of Hecate Triformis, and so to have been forbidden eternally to blush unseen, as no doubt they now desire to do. It would be prudent, also, to wait a while before conferring diplomas of immortality upon the heroes of legislation. The fame of repealers of navigation laws and founders of household franchise should be considered as in a state of pupilage for at least fifty years; and they should not be allowed to sport bronze thighs and the *toga virilis*, before the public buildings or in the squares of the metropolis, ere the paper on which their Bills are printed is well dry. It should be remembered that, in our haste, we may be placing an awful and easy vengeance in the hands of posterity; which might choose, not to pull down such monuments, but—to let them stand.

But of all modes of premature insistence upon the verdict of fame, that which is most to be avoided, if we would avoid making ourselves unnecessarily absurd, is that of decreeing immortality during or soon after their lifetime to literary men and artists. If, indeed, there existed academies of art and literature, which should consist of all the best men of their kind, all actuated by the most disinterested appreciation of merit not their ownin their own profession, then we might have some approximation—but only an approximation—to a safe tribunal; and if Smith and his friends were such boobies as to want the cake of fame before it was baked, Smith might be "busted up" in the Abbey, or obtain a parliamentary guarantee of being puff-worthy, in his own day or immediately after, with little more to be said against it than that it was a want of decorum, all the more disgusting on account of the dignity of the occasion and the absence of any call for hurry. But, as no such academy could exist, or, if it existed, could make its decrees prevail with those who are the decreers of statues, how does the matter stand? A man who has done his best, perhaps, to give us harmless amusement, and whose only crime is that of having succeeded too well in adapting himself to the poor capacities and passing moods of his present audience, is now in such danger as he never was at any former time of finding himself rewarded with ten thousand per annum here and an eternity of contempt hereafter.

If persons of culture and natural taste have often to confess that the painter or poet or novelist whose muse was the seemingly faultless mistress of his affections five-and-twenty years ago, now stands before him as a false Duessa, what should we think of the right to raise monuments claimed by thatpublic which is as changeable in its tastes as it is liberal in paying for their indulgence? Yet it is this public that is venturing more and more audaciously to anticipate the verdict of time. True, it often uses a Minister or a committee of experts as its agent, councillor, and representative; but it is none the safer for that. If the agents themselves know better, they know the value of their own popularity too well to say so; or they may have a secret grudge against Smith, and so cry "Ay" with all their hearts when the people ask, "Shall Smith have a statue?"

XXII

IDEAL AND MATERIAL GREATNESS IN ARCHITECTURE

ST. THOMAS AQUINAS writes, "Great riches are not required for the habit of magnificence; it is enough that a man should dispose of such as he possesses greatly, according to time and place." As in life, so in art, and especially in architecture, greatness of style is quite independent of wealth of material; indeed, wealth of material is constantly found by true artists to be a fatal hindrance to grandeur of effect. Hence great poets and painters are usually very shy of what commonly pass for great subjects—that is, subjects full of obvious interest and splendour; and, if they treat such subjects at all, they begin by denuding them as far as possible of all that makes them attractive to the novice in art, until they come to a simple greatness which was hitherto a secret.

Now I wish to point out what I conceive to be a principal condition of great effect with small means and in small or comparatively small buildings. It is magnificence in the expenditure of such material as the architect possesses, and especially of stone, brick, and timber. It is commonly supposed, even by architects, that a solidity of wall and roof sufficient to put far out of sight any idea of insecurity or decay, if properly shown forth and expressed by chamfer, moulding, cornice, shafted recess, and the many other "decorations" which are principally methods of showing the thickness of wall and weight of roof, is all that noble building calls for; and that the frequent—nay, general—practice of ancient architecture in going much further than this was simply waste of material caused by want of mechanical knowledge. But those who know most of ancient architecture know best that there was no want of mechanical knowledge displayed in it, but quite the reverse. Not only is mechanical knowledge, equal if not beyond our own, proved by such buildings as York and Salisbury Cathedrals, but the house and cottage builder of the sixteenth and seventeenth centuries seems to have known all the details of his business fully as well as the most ingenious economist of material that ever "scamped" a modern tenement of the same order. He was fully aware that the strength of a rafter lay rather in its depth than its breadth, and that, for a time at least, a few boards two inches thick and ten inches deep, set edgeways, would suffice to carry the roof, which nevertheless it pleased him better to lay upon a succession of beams ten inches square. It is the reality, and the modest ostentation of the reality, of such superfluous substantiality that constitutes the whole secret of effect in many an old house that strikes us as "architectural" though it may not contain a single item of architectural ornament; and, in the very few instances in which modern buildings have been raised in the same fashion, the beholder at once feels that their generous regard for the far future is of almost as poetical a character as the aged retrospect of a similar house of the time of Henry VII or Elizabeth. A man now hires a bit of ground for eighty or ninety years; and, if he has something to spare to spend on beauty, he says to himself: "I will build me a house that will last my time, and what money I have over I will spend in decorating it. Why should I waste my means in raising wall and roof which will last five times as long as I or mine shall want them?" The answer is: Because that very "waste" is the truest and most striking ornament; and though you and your family's usufruct of a house thus magnanimously built may be but a fifth of its natural age, there lies in that very fact an "ornament" of the most noble and touching kind, which will be obvious at all seasons to yourself and every beholder, though the consciousness of its cause may be dormant; whereas the meanness of your own plan will be only the more apparent with every penny you spend in making it meretricious.

I have said that a modest *ostentation* of extreme substantiality is also an element of architectural effect in the kind of building contemplated. This, indeed, is the properly architectural or artistic element. A house will look respectable, and something more than respectable, which has only the reality of being built somewhat better than well. But consciousness is the life of art, and there must be a quiet rejoicing in strength, solidity, and permanence, to give these characters that power over the imagination which a work of art must have. A labourer's cottage or the smallest village church which has this character is an artistic and rightly architectural work; and the nobleman's mansion or the cathedral which wants it is not. Here comes in that true "decoration" which scarcely the humblest house of the sixteenth or early part of the seventeenth century was altogether without. In out-of-the-way villages and roadside inns of that period, you will find your attention directed to the thickness and weight of the roof-timbers by a carved or moulded cornice, which measures and expatiates upon the depth and substance of the rafters which terminate therein; or one or more of the brackets supporting the joists of the overhanging bedroom floor will have a touch of carving, to declare with what ease and pleasure the burthen is borne upon their sturdy shoulders; or the lintel of the door will show and boast of the thickness of the wall by a moulded chamfer. A single touch of such decoration glorifies the whole, and puts the living spirit of art into the body of an honest building, however humble it may be.

So far is size from being needful to greatness in architecture, that one of the very grandest pieces of domestic building I ever saw is a little village inn of extremely early date in a Sussex village which scarcely anybody has ever heard of, though it stands but two miles from Berwick Station on the South Coast Railway. This village is Aldfriston. It has in its little market-place an extremely ancient stone cross, far gone in decay, having never been touched by restorer. The whole village has an air of antiquity such as breathes from no other English village I have ever seen; but older than anything, except the cross, is its hostelry—no bigger than a well-to-do bailiff's cottage, showing no Elizabethan "variety" in its ground-plan, and the front to the street having but three windows above and one on either side of the doorway. Coming upon it quite unprepared for seeing anything particular in the village, this house fairly took my breath away by its exemplification of the way in which ideal and material greatness differ. It was like coming, in a newspaper article, upon three or four lines of great and unknown poetry. Yet it was nothing but a cottage built mightily, and with a mighty consciousness of being so built. It seems never to have been touched, except here and there by the house-painter, since the date at which it was raised, which was probably in the fifteenth century, the carved foliage in the spandrels of the small arched doorway indicating that period. An architect learned in mouldings might perhaps fix the date to within twenty-five years, from those of the cornice. The bedroom story projects considerably over the ground-floor, and is borne by great oak brackets, the faces of which are adorned with painted carvings of figures in mitres, one being St. Hubert, as is shown by the stag at his feet. The spaces between these brackets are ceiled with a great plaster "cavetto," which, together with the brackets, springs from a wide timber cornice above the door and windows of the ground-floor. In the hollow of this cornice are four or five grotesque faces, the painting of which, though fresh, seems, like the painting of all the other decorations, to be nothing but the original colouring faithfully transmitted. The three windows of the upper floor are bays, and are carried by great spread brackets, carved and painted with most curiously quaint and simple representations of St. George and the Dragon and symbols of his tradition, the tails of two dragons in the central bracket running in their extremities into the outlines of a pointed and foliated arch. The roof is covered in with slabs of ragged stone, thick enough for a London pavement. The dimensions of the timbers of the roof are proved inferentially by the fact that the roof-tree has not sagged an inch under some four hundred years of this burthen; and their mass and power are expressed artistically by their termination in a cornice of immense depth, and consisting of a greater number of moulded "members" than I remember to have seen in any other feature of the kind. The walls are plastered in their plain spaces, but indicate their construction of solid oak—

which, by the way, is far more durable than either brick or any ordinary stone—by the chance appearance in one place of a strange animal which runs up the face of the wall and is obviously carved out of a beam otherwise hid by the plaster.

There is nothing heavy in the total effect of this extraordinary piece of cottage architecture; for there is artistic animation everywhere, and the expression of its strength is that of living power and not mere passive sufficiency.

To build such a cottage now might cost about three times as much as it does to build a common country inn of the same dimensions. It would not, of course, suit a London citizen so well as a Chiselhurst villa of like size and cost; but it would be a fit abode for a duke in difficulties.

XXIII

"OLD ENGLISH" ARCHITECTURE, ANCIENT AND MODERN

THE style of architecture in which the great majority of country houses, and very many town houses, from the cottage to the mansion, have been built during the past fifteen years, is a very great improvement upon the nameless mode—for which no better title could be invented than the "factory style"—which prevailed in house architecture during great part of last century and the first half of this. And it is a yet greater improvement upon the falsification of that simple though sordid way of building, by attempting to change its misery into magnificence by "compo" mockeries of stone construction and a style of ornament created to express the thickness of the wall or the weight of roof of a Renaissance palace. Most persons are contented with describing the improved mode as Old English, fancying that it is a real return to the way in which houses were built in the reign of Elizabeth or James or thereabouts. But there is a notable distinction between ancient and modern "Old English." It is this: the "variety" in form which is of the essence of the last was but the accident of the first. Whitehall and the Parthenon are not more simply symmetrical in their masses than are many of the finest specimens of Early English domestic architecture; and the "variety" which we moderns suppose we are copying is, in nearly all cases, either the result of change of plan in the process of building, or of subsequent additions by which the original symmetry was sacrificed. That the sacrifice was often without loss, and often even a gain—as such a sacrifice could never be in the case of a Greek or Renaissance building—is owing to the fact that domesticity is the central thought and expression of the one kind of architecture and public ostentation of the other. Accordingly, the keynote of an Early English house is its stack of chimneys, upon which it was considered impossible to lavish too much ornament. From the cottage of the Sussex labourer to the great nobleman's mansion—such as that most exquisite of all existing specimens of Tudor building, "Compton in the Hole"—the chimneys are the things which first attract the eye and delight it longest; whereas the Greek, Roman, or Renaissance house is heartily ashamed of its smoke, and has never yet succeeded thoroughly in dealing with its disgrace. Symmetry, then, in the old country house was looked upon as good; but convenience and comfort, and the expression of convenience and comfort, better. Now, in a house well and deliberately planned for the convenience of any household, large or small, the ground-plan and elevation will be naturally simple and symmetrical; simplicity, too, is economical, and economy a part of domesticity. Accordingly, the great Tudor mansions and palaces of England, the builders of which could have best afforded to pay for the supposed charm of "variety," are, for the most part, the simplest in plan and elevation; while it is in the ill-planned and often-added-to village inn or rectory that the vagaries of "variety," so alluring to the modern mind, are almost exclusively found.

In Old English architecture this variety is a very real though accidental beauty. It has the double charm of intensifying the primary expression of domesticity by the very sense of the sacrifice which has been made to it, and of giving the building, however small, a touch of historical character. But what if these beauties of the old architecture are sought to be obtained in the modern by sacrifices of convenience, economy, and domesticity, and by a deliberate planning of structural "after-thoughts," or subsequent necessities, from the beginning! What if a house, full of small and uncomfortable rooms connected, or rather isolated, by mazes of dark staircases, landings, and passages, has been manifestly built at one blow, and at twice the cost at which a simple and symmetrical and scarcely less— nay, to the initiated, more—beautiful house of the same period of architecture might have been built, without the sacrifice of any modern convenience? Surely, if the devil were an architect his "favourite sin" would be this kind of "cottage of gentility."

The "variety" of a real Old English house is not only nearly always the outcome of some convenience or necessity discovered or arising after the first building of it, but is nearly always obviously so. Some little difference of style not too great to break harmony, will indicate a difference of date; or it will be shown by some infraction of the lines of the original building. The library or parlour which cuts off a return of the label of the pantry window is manifestly an addition. But it would be too ridiculous to copy such proofs of accident and alteration into a nineteenth-century rectory, villa, or mansion; and the consequence is, that to an understanding eye its variety is often in appearance, as it is in reality, mere imbecility aping the movements of reason.

There is no real anachronism in the revival of the ordinary details of Old English house architecture, though there is sometimes in that of the material. The "half-timbered" wall belongs only to times and places in which bricks and tiles are not to be had, and in which abundance of the best oak timber is. But hooded gables, deep cornices, bracketed bays, weather-tiled walls, the projection of upper over lower stories, and almost all the other charming features of the mode, have sound reasons of use which hold as good now as they did in the year 1600; and in these reasons alone consists their architectural charm. The characteristic Old English chimney—the most ornamental feature of the style—has its full justification in use; the loading of the top with projecting layer after layer of bricks, laid even or notch-wise, forming that security against hurricane which is so often sought, in the "factory" style, by the one or more long iron rods which agreeably break the sky-line of many modern mansions. Even the scalloped tile, which so often replaces the square in old weather-tiled walls, has its utilitarian purpose—a saving of material; the greatest breadth of the scallop being superposed upon the juncture of the tiles below, so as to protect it from wet. The projection, in a long low house of the modest rectory or farmhouse type, of the bedroomstory over the basement is the feature farthest of all from being merely ornamental. In such a house more space was usually wanted for bedrooms than for living-rooms and offices, and a very moderate projection of the upper story supplies this additional space.

XXIV

ARCHITECTURAL STYLES

I

Every one has a perfectly definite impression of what is meant by an architectural style; and would recognise a building as Egyptian, Greek, Ecclesiastical Gothic, Norman, or Moresque, not merely by the characteristic details of each of these manners, but still more by a perfectly distinct character attained in each manner by the combination of those details—a character which is totally different from any effect that could result from any such random though more or less constant collocation of details as is to be found, for example, in the bastard "Italian Gothic." This, though it was made popular by Mr. Ruskin, has about as much relation to a true style as a curiosity-shop has to a well-ordered living-room. It is a remarkable fact, and one especially worth dwelling upon in this context, that Italy, thecountry of the arts, never had an architecture, and could never even adopt one from its neighbours without degrading or abolishing its character as a style. The so-called "Romanesque" was an incongruous hybrid until it was developed into the "Norman" by the northern nations of Europe; and though the pointed arch made its appearance in Italy very early, no Italian architect ever seems to have had any perception of its artistic capacity, even when he adopted in his buildings the constructive system to which that feature belonged. Italy had great architects, but no great architecture. Buildings like St. Mark's, the Doge's Palace, the Duomo of Florence, etc., owe their influence upon the imagination to the personality of the architect, which has known how to impress itself on a combination of in themselves unmeaning or incongruous forms, rather than to that imaginative integrity of style which makes every Old English parish church look as if the Spirit had built its own house. Every great architect—like every great poet, painter, or musician—has his own style, whether he works on the lines of a great integral style like the Northern Pointed, or in a mongrel mode like that of the Romanesque, or in no accepted manner at all. Sir Christopher Wren could not build a common brick house without imposing his own character upon it.But this personal character or style, which always marks the work of the great artist, is usually almost beyond the power of analysis; and, were it otherwise, would scarcely be worth the trouble of analysis, which would only serve the purpose of encouraging imitations of that which owes its value to its unique individuality.

The five styles above named—*i.e.* the Egyptian, the Greek, the Pointed Gothic, the Norman, and the Moresque—are so much distinguished from all other modes of building by the integrity with which a single idea is carried out in every detail, that in comparison with them there is no other manner which deserves to be called a style. And it is hard to conjecture the possibility of the development in the future of any sixth style which shall deserve to rank with them; for these five seem to have exhausted the five possible modes in which weight or mass of material—apparently the foundations of all architectural expression—can be treated. Two of these styles, the Norman and the Moresque, though equal to the others in artistic integrity, are immeasurably inferior to them in significance; the first three having dealt with and exhausted the only modes in which the primary fact of weight of material in stone construction can be subordinated to religious expression, and the field itself of religious expression inarchitecture having been in like manner cleared by these styles: for when the Material, the Rational, and the Spiritual have once found utterance in stone—as they have done in the temple-architectures of Egypt, Greece, and Northern Europe—what fourth religious aspect remains to inspire a new art?

It is proposed in these papers to consider the several expressional themes of the five great architectures, and to give a brief exposition of the way in which they are worked out. It should be premised, however, that as it does not require a knowledge of how an effect is produced in order to feel that effect, so it is not pretended that any very distinct consciousness of the adaptation of means to expressional ends must have existed in the minds of the inventors of the great styles of architecture. All artistic production involves a large element of lucky accident, of which the true artist alone knows how to avail himself; and it is often from a lucky accident in a happy season that a great work or a great art will take its origin, as the dropping of a grain of sand into a saturated solution of certain salts will form the centre and cause of its sudden crystallisation. As sound philosophy is only sound sense spread out, so true criticism of great work is only right perception spread out; and the use of criticism ofsuch work is not so much to teach men to enjoy it, as to enable them to pronounce a prompt and assured and demonstrable condemnation of bad or inferior work when false or exaggerated claims are put forth in its favour.

The three primary architectures seem to have owed their origin to three accidents. The immense and wholly unreasonable massiveness which characterises the Egyptian style is probably due to its having emerged from caverns. It carried into the air its memory of having had the rocky earth for its roof and walls, and of the time when its close-packed squadrons of granite shafts were a necessity which it cost nothing to provide. The

Parthenon, again, is a manifest glorification in stone of the forms of the wooden hut; and the pointed arch, with all its immense consequences, arose from the constructional accident of cross-vaulting.

Weight, then, which is the most general and characteristic attribute of matter, was taken by the Egyptian, Greek, and Gothic architects as the ground of their several ideas—whether consciously or not, is no concern of ours. The Egyptian architect, as will be shown, subordinated every detail, from the mass of the pyramid—which may be regarded as the form taken by weight in the abstract—down to almost every particular of decoration, to the creation of an effect of compulsory submission to an irresistible and for-ever-enduring material power. The mightiest bulk of Alp or Apennine is a bubble compared with an Egyptian temple, which is the awful *life* of ponderosity and crushing earthliness; and there is no need to pause in order to point out how aptly this expression suited the political and religious character of the people out of whom Israel fled.

In the architecture of Greece, weight—representative of material force—was still the theme; but it was material force which had met with its match, the force of mind; and the ponderous entablature, every detail of which expresses weight, is lifted and borne beautifully in air by a series of members every one of which conveys the impression of an opposite ascendant force, which recognises but does not suffer in the least degree from its burthen, beneath which the animated shaft is seen to fling away a part of its supporting power just at the point where most weight is borne, and the Caryatides of the Pandrosium can afford to stand with one knee bent easily forward. Here, then, again was a great and new phase of the human mind envisaging the universe, expressed by simple reference to weight of material in its temples.

The third great phase—that in which an asceticspirituality, refusing all willing alliance with earthliness, only recognises it as a thing to be defied and to be made the measure of the spirit's predominance—obtained its artistic expression by employing material weight as the symbol of its opponent; which it neither suffers from nor enters into alliance with, but vanquishes, converts, and glorifies in ascending streams of life.

The Moresque style also owes its singular integrity of effect to a peculiar mode of regarding the idea of gravitation: if that can be called a mode of regarding it which consists in a most ingenious and fanciful ignoring of it, either as an oppressor, an ally, or a vanquished foe. The honeycombed domes of the Alhambra and the Mosque of Cordova hang apparently suspended in air upon "pendentives," like sunny clouds in station; and the astonishing art by which innumerable details are made to concur in this effect would justify this style in ranking with the three foregoing, had this effect any symbolic meaning for the human race and its religions; but it has no meaning for men who have their feet upon the earth, and is only adapted for the palaces and temples of a race of sylphs or gnomes.

Lastly, the Norman style, though no less consistent an exponent of one idea than are the other temple styles, is founded upon no reference tosuperincumbent weight, but depends almost wholly upon its boast of the mass and eternal stability of the wall. It well conveys the solemn expression of a calm eternity of time; but for religious purposes it will not bear the least comparison with the flamelike Gothic, expressing at once the peace and ardour of the "eternal moment."

In the following papers a short analysis will be given of the somewhat obscure means by which the well-recognised expressions of these five great architectures are obtained.

II

The symbolisation of material life and power by an elaborately artistic treatment of the mere fact of weight, which is the most universal and obvious attribute of matter, is the object of every general form and of almost every, so-called decorative, detail of Egyptian architecture; the few exceptions, such as the occasional intrusion of the lotus and palm into the capitals of the columns, being due to an obscure but probably intimately related symbolism of a different kind.

The pyramid is the simplest artistic form by which mere weight can be expressed. It is nothing more nor less than a mound or mountain shapedso as to give it an artistic consciousness. The form of the Egyptian Temple is nothing but the expression of this elementary form of weight with emphasis upon emphasis, until there results such an accumulation and concentration of the idea of weight that the whole building seems as if it would crush the earth on which it stands. This effect is mainly produced by a multiplication of the pyramidal form in the masses of the building; by its truncation at various heights, which introduces the powerful element of suggestion; by numerous inferior members which emphasise the expression by contrast; and by such a multiplication and formation of shaft and capital as to convey the idea of an overwhelming burthen above them. The great double-towered Propylon of the typical Egyptian Temple is, in its entire mass, a truncated pyramid; and, as simply such, is a much more forcible expression of pyramidal form than the pyramid itself. This expression is doubled by the division of the upper part of the mass into two low towers. Immense *cavetto* cornices crown these towers, and intensify their effect by the strongest contrast. Their pyramidal outline is emphasised to the eye by the great roll-mouldings which follow the angles of the masonry from summit to base. Finally, the plane of the great doorway by which the two masses of the Propylon are joined leavesthat of the pyramidal mass and becomes nearly perpendicular, while the sides of the doorway become actually perpendicular—constituting a *cumulative* contrast which seems to double the already manifold emphasis of the main bulk of the building. The comparatively low mass of the body of the temple behind the Propylon is still the truncated pyramid crowned with the contrasting cornice; but the truncation occurs so near the ground, and so far from what would be the apex were the converging lines of wall continued upwards, that the pyramidal form would scarcely have been suggested, were it not for its plainer manifestation in the Propylon; but, with this aid, the eye at once catches the idea of the decapitated pyramid throughout. Through openings in these strongly inclined walls appeared the vertical colonnades; and such niches or apertures as were practised in these walls had the contrast of perpendicular jambs. In front of the vast ponderosity of the Egyptian Temple rose the final and most effective contrast to the whole—the "fingers of the sun": the pair of tall and slender monoliths, which only tapered sufficiently to give them the reality and the appearance of security. In the interior of the building the idea of weight had to be conveyed in a different manner—namely, by the bulk, number, and form of the columns.Every detail of shaft and capital—with the two or three exceptions already spoken of—was calculated to express actual sufferance from the burthen borne by them. The shafts bulge towards the base, and the capitals likewise swell as they approach their juncture with the shafts; shaft and capital being usually clothed with vertical convex mouldings: the exact reverse of the Doric shaft, which, as will be shown, had exactly the opposite idea to convey. Unlike the repose and sufficiency of the Doric column, the Egyptian expresses violent and yet insufficient energy, which seems to rush towards and to be partially driven back by the entablature. The immense thickness of wall, wherever it was shown, was emphasised by sculpture in very low relief. These are only the main elements of an effect which, and the means of producing which, will be more forcibly felt by a corresponding analysis of Greek architecture, which culminates in the Doric of the Parthenon.

This temple has a double basement, the first of which is on a "dead level"; from this rises the second basement, in which the true life of the building commences. In 1837 Mr. Pennethorne announced the important discovery that the lines of this basement, together with those of the entablature, are not horizontal lines, but parabolic curves; and Mr. Penrose, in 1852, in a workpublished by the Society of Dilettanti, gave the actual measurements of these curves; which are found to prevail not only in the horizontal but in all the vertical lines and faces, in the inclined lines of the pediment, and in the axes of the shafts. These curves are so subtle—the rise being only an inch or two in as many hundred feet—that they are rather felt than seen; but that they are felt, even by the comparatively gross modern eye, is clear enough from the different way in which it is affected by the Parthenon itself and by any imitation of it by modern builders. It is probable that these curves were in some instances meant to correct optical illusions, by which straight lines would look hollow, etc.; but a far greater motive for their introduction was an effect of animation in the whole and in every part and of unity through the predominance of general curves, which a cultivated eye can discern very easily, but which is probably beyond our present powers of analysis. Above the basement the Doric Temple externally—and the Greek Temple's architectural beauty is all outside—consists of two parts, of opposite and exactly balanced significance. The first consists of a colonnade of shafts, each of which rises at once from the stylobate, without the footing or "base" found in subsequent styles. The shaft diminishes somewhat rapidly, until it impingesupon and ends in the capital; which is an hyperbolic "ovolo," spreading widely under the "abacus" or tile, which constitutes the neutral point, or point of rest, between the column and the entablature. The outlines of the shaft (always fluted in early Greek architecture) converge from the base towards the capital—not in straight lines, but in decided parabolic curves, of which the departure from straight lines is greatest at about two-thirds of the height of the shaft. This curve of the shaft is called the *entasis*; and upon it depends mainly the expressional life of the shaft. It will be remembered that there is a similar swelling in the Egyptian shaft; but this is where it approaches the base. Its position in the Greek shaft expresses an ascendant energy of force, which is manifested most strongly as it approaches the capital. In the one case yielding under weight is expressed, in the other superabundant power. This animated expression is multiplied by every multiplication of the outline provided by the flutings, which in the Greek shaft are concave, expressing concentration of force towards the centre; whereas, in the Egyptian the flutings are convex, expressing further a tendency to bulge and burst under their burthen. A little under the capital, and just where the Greek shaft is thinnest, one or more deep channels are incised in itssubstance, showing that power can be triumphantly cast away just where power is most needed. The Egyptian shaft, at the same point, is usually bound with a heavy thonglike moulding, as if to prevent it from being crushed. The ovolo, which constitutes the Doric capital, provides and expresses the distribution of the power of the shaft to meet the superincumbent entablature; and the "quirk" or sudden diminution of its breadth immediately under the abacus is a repetition of the device of the incised channels for proving the existence of superabundant power. At the point where the Greek entablature is met with easy grace by the noble spread of the hyperbolic ovolo, the Egyptian capital, as a rule, diminishes and seems to dash itself with violence towards the point of conflict.

As every feature of the column thus expresses cheerful and abundant energy, every detail of the entablature is a mode of expressing the weight which is thus met and carried with such graceful power. The Doric entablature is made up of three parts—architrave, frieze, and cornice—each expressing in a different manner the idea of weight. The architrave is a massive layer of stone with its face unbroken by any sort of "decoration"; it projects beyond the neck of the shaft, so that a line dropped from it would about touch the outer circumference of the shaft at its base. In thismember, then, weight is expressed by a simple mass directly imposed upon the centres of support. The frieze is a similar layer of masonry having its face broken up by triglyphs—members resembling, and no doubt originating in, the terminations of beams of timber. These triglyphs are slightly projecting quadrilateral masses of stone, considerably higher than they are broad, and cut into deep vertical channels. They would express little besides the memory of the old timber construction, were it not for the *guttæ* which hang below them, separated from them by a fillet. These guttæ, by multiplying the vertical lines of the triglyphs, confer upon them the appearance of pendants, the force of the earthward tendency being increased by the fillets, whose momentary interruption of that tendency seems to increase it. To increase what Franz Kugler calls the "triglyphic character," little pendants sometimes occur at the top of the chamfered sides of the triglyphs. No one can realise the whole force of this extremely simple means of expression except by trying what the Doric entablature would be without it. There is, or was, a church in the Waterloo Road, massively built and preserving pretty well all the features of the Doric Temple, except the triglyphs and guttæ. Their omission makes the whole building light-headed. There seems to be no meaning inthe vast current of upward force in the fluted shafts, if that is all they have to carry. Any one can satisfy himself of this point by simply covering the frieze, in a print of a Doric Temple, by a slip of white paper. Of course this all-important triglyphic character, though only expressed in the frieze, is felt to apply to the entire mass of the entablature, of which the weight is thus *made visible*.

As the architrave expresses simple weight, and the frieze weight depending, so the cornice is weight impending. The great projection of this massive member beyond the face of the frieze and architrave contains in itself the ground of that expression; but it is carefully heightened by the deep undercutting of the corona, which throws the mass forward and separates it by a dark shadow from the top of the frieze; and it is still further heightened by a repetition of the rows of guttæ—which, however, in this instance seem to be sliding off the inclined faces of the mutules (inclined slabs set in the undercutting of the corona); so that the same device which gives dependent weight in the frieze, expresses weight impendent in the cornice.

These are only a few of the more obvious means by which the lovely equilibrium of the Doric style is created. There are many other details which it is impossible to notice here; but every one bearsthe central thought constantly in view, and adds to the most perfect—though not perhaps the highest—architectural beauty which the world has ever seen. The other so-called "orders" are only modifications or corruptions of the same idea.

III

Before proceeding to show how the idea of Greek architecture, symbolised in a system of construction and decoration which emphasised to the eye in every detail an exact adequacy of endeavour to effect, was modified or corrupted in the so-called "Ionic," "Corinthian," and other "orders," a few words should be said about the very peculiar and little understood treatment of the wall by the Doric architects. As a contrast to the active conflict of apparently ascending power in the columns with the gravitating power, rendered, as it were, visible in the entablature, the treatment of the walls of the *naos, pronaos,* and *posticum*—that is, of the body of the temple and of the porches created by the prolongation of the side walls—is emphatically passive and neutral, and just the reverse of the treatment of the wall by the Egyptians, who made it the base of a truncated pyramid, a mass of conscious ponderosity, which "lean'd down on earth with all its weight." The vertical junctures of the stones of the walls of the Greek Temple were rendered invisible by polishing their adjacent faces; but the horizontal faces were rough-worked, so that the wall-face presented a series of straight lines parallel to the base. These lines were only strong enough to be plainly seen, through the gaps in that torrent of ascending power, the fluted colonnade; increasing that force by their contrast, but themselves expressing nothing but the fact that the wall was a wall, built in ordinary courses of masonry. Had the perpendicular junctures of the masonry been visible, the contrast to the shafts—which were either monoliths or had the junctures of the *frustra* so polished that they looked like monoliths—would have been lost. The *antæ*, or ends of the walls, are treated in a way which is particularly noteworthy. In the Roman corruptions of Greek architecture these antæ were confused with and often treated as flattened and applied shafts. The fact of passive resistance of the wall, in contrast to the active resistance of the colonnade, is carefully but very unobtrusively expressed in these wall-terminations in the purest Doric. Where the strongly ascending force of the shaft sacrifices power in order to prove its abundance, the antæ are increased in breadth andstrength by successive cappings, or by mouldings so undercut as to express a rolling over or sufferance from superimposed weight; there is no *entasis* or visible swell in the antæ—until they were used by later architects who had lost the sense of what entasis meant; these wall-terminations were further strengthened by a base, which no Doric shaft ever had. The base and capping were, more or less, continued along the top and bottom of the whole wall, the doors and other apertures of which usually diminished in width towards the top, suggesting—but still in a passive and unobtrusive way—the simple reality of weight and pressure in the wall, and affording a further and most important contrast to the living "emporstreben," as the German critics call it, of the line of shafts. Thus Mr. Ruskin is wrong in saying that "in the Greek Temple the wall is as nothing; the entire interest is in the detached columns and the frieze (entablature?) they bear." The wall is the expression of the passive life that becomes active when it is concentrated in the colonnade, and has so much more work to do.

In the "Ionic Order" exactly the same idea of the symbolisation of the balance of material and intellectual forces is carried out with the same integrity as in the Doric, though with less simplicity and obviousness. The idea of elasticity—asnoticed by Franz Kugler in his *Handbuch der Kunstgeschichte* for the first time—is added to that of simple upward met by simple downward force. It occurs especially in the base and the volutes of the column, as these members are found modified and perfected by the Attic architects. By tracing the growth of the Attic base, much light will be thrown upon the Greek architectural idea. A base is a support for the shaft. The Doric had no base, because the notion of any weight to be supported was not allowed to be expressed anywhere but in the entablature; the Ionic differing from the Doric mainly in this—that the visible conflict between weight and supporting power, which in the Doric was wholly concentrated upon the abacus, or tile, where the column met the entablature, was in the Ionic so distributed that almost every member was at once agent and reagent, expressing an adequate power of supporting what was above it, but also requiring support from that which was below. A great square stone or plinth is the simplest form of base; but this would have looked poor and inorganic underneath the elaborately fluted and voluted column. The square stone cut into a circle with its edges rounded is the next simplest form; but it was left for the Romans to use this base, for they had not the sensitive eye that discerned the fataleffect of swelling or sufferance from weight which this cushion-like form conveys. The first Ionic base had a *scotia*, or hollow receding moulding, under the round *torus*. This contradicted the above impression; but it did it violently and awkwardly. Finally, the Attic base was formed of a large torus below, a smaller one above, and the scotia, or receding moulding, between them; so that the base—which, on the whole, was a spreading and supporting member—was nevertheless narrowest where it would have been thickest had it suffered, like a cushion, from the weight it carried. The fluting of the Ionic order, while it expressed ascendant force like the Doric, had a flat space or fillet instead of a sharp edge between each concavity, and each line of fluting had semicircular terminations. The effect of this was to endow the shaft itself with a substantive expression of weight, which had no existence in the Doric shaft, that flew, like a sheaf of arrows, from the earth to strike against the ovolo of the capital. The Ionic capital, like the Ionic base, had its elastic character perfectly developed by Attic architects. In the original Ionic the ears of the volutes simply hang on either side of the ovolo like horns; but in Attic specimens they appear to be formed by the pressure of the entablature upon a series of elastic curves. The Ionic abacus differs from the Doric in expressing, in common with all the other members of the Ionic column, an active supporting power; whereas the Doric tile is simply negative, the "point of rest" between the opposing forces of the column and entablature. The architrave, the first member of the Ionic entablature, instead of expressing weight by simple mass, as the Doric architrave does, consists of two or three layers of masonry, the upper projecting over the other, and giving to the entire entablature the expression of impending weight, which in the Doric is limited to the corona. In the frieze there are no guttæ or triglyphs, because the pendent effect which these give to the Doric frieze would be inconsistent with the continuation of the idea of support as well as weight throughout all the members of the Ionic order. In the pure Doric there is absolutely no such thing as ornament; though Kugler, notwithstanding that he is of all critics the one who has come nearest to the perception of the true sense of Greek architecture, asserts that the head and foot members of the antæ are merely ornamental. How far this is from being the case has been now shown. The so-called "egg and arrow" and other figures into which Greek mouldings were cut have nothing to do with ornament. They are simply the means of emphasising the forms of the mouldings and rendering them visible at distances at which otherwise they would not be distinguished. But in the Ionic we have real architectural ornament, and lines of roses or bands of foliage are inserted at points where it is desirable to express—in the absence of more severe means of expression—the freedom and cheerfulness with which a superincumbent weight is carried.

The "Corinthian" is only a highly decorated Ionic, and the Greeks of the good age seem to have thought it fittest for secular or semi-secular purposes. It only attained somewhat of the character of an "Order" in the hands of the Romans, who had little taste for or understanding of pure Greek art, but had sufficient intelligence to see how to apply ornament for the most part in the right places. When they tried to improve upon the Doric of the Parthenon, they did it in a very characteristic way. They simplified it by doing away with the fluting of the shaft and setting it upon a base of the single torus or roll-moulding, so that it looked like a big sausage set on end upon a small curly one; and instead of the channel cut in the neck of the shaft—which must have been a hopeless puzzle to them—they bound the shaft at the same point with a projecting moulding: as the Egyptians did rightly, because they wanted to express an idea the exact opposite of the Greek one. Meretricious ornament and mock simplicity went hand in hand, and all pretensions to integrity of style had to be abandoned when the arch and the entablature had to be reconciled. As builders the Romans perhaps surpassed all others before or since; and as architects also they were as great as they could be, in the absence of the Greek devotion to the unity produced by one all-pervading symbolic thought.

IV

The pointed Gothic, though it took its rise more than fifteen hundred years after the decay of Attic architecture, and after the intervention of several other styles, of which the "Norman" constitutes one of the five great and only pure styles which the world has seen, is nevertheless in closer artistic relationship with the Attic style than the Norman is, and should be therefore treated earliest. The immense effort which was made to develop a great style from the dome—the natural outcome of the circular arch introduced by the Romans—never came to anything but the production of here and there an edifice which, like the Pantheon and St. Sophia, were miracles of technical skill, until the idea was taken up by the fanciful Moresque architects. Again, the Norman, though a great integral style, as will be shown, is not based upon any relation to weight of material; which is at once the great fact of building, and as such is made by the Egyptian, Greek, and Gothic architects to express the material, intellectual, and spiritual character of worship in ways that exhaust this primary source of architectural symbolism.

Weight—simple and irresistible in the Egyptian, adequately supported in the Greek—is, in the pointed Gothic, not abolished as in the Moresque, but totally vanquished and borne above, as by a superior spiritual power. Two happy accidents gave rise to this architectural development. As the Egyptian architecture was an artistic transfiguration of the necessities of an original cavern architecture, and as the Doric Temple in a similar way transmuted to undreamt-of significance the forms of the timber hut, so the Gothic architecture found in the Basilica—the main forms of which were transmitted through the Norman cathedral—the accidental key to what probably will for ever remain the supreme glory of the art of temple-building. The Basilica itself contained nothing but the discovery of the most convenient way of roofing-in and lighting a great oblong hall. It consisted of nave and aisles; the walls of the nave rising within and above those of the aisles, to form the clerestory, which gave the centre of the edifice externally the appearance of unsheathing itself from and soaring above the rest. The means of emphasising and multiplying this effect indefinitely—as the pyramidal effect was multiplied and emphasised in the Egyptian Temple—were provided by another fortunate accident, the development of the pointed arch from the mechanical necessities of cross-vaulting. No sooner did a row of pointed arches make its appearance in the clerestory windows than the power of Gothic expression, latent in the main body of the building, became obvious. The tower, with its spire, was the first and simplest sequence. It was to the clerestory what this was to the main body of the building. In the course of a few years every detail of construction and decoration became subordinated to the heavenward flight which the main masses of the building had thus taken.

This fact is a threadbare commonplace of architectural criticism, and one which is obvious to the eye of the dullest beholder of the interior or exterior of every Gothic cathedral; but the number and subtlety of the means by which the effect is gained is beyond all reckoning and analysis; and the object of this paper is to point out only a fewof them which are not to be found in architectural manuals, and to show how this all-prevailing stream of ardent aspiration was moderated and governed so as to acquire the expression of peace as well as ardour, as befitted the beauty of the Christian temple. Mr. Freeman comes nearer than any other eminent architectural critic to a clear discernment of Gothic character when he says: "Where there is no strife there is no victory; the vertical line cannot be called predominant unless the horizontal exist in a visible condition of subjection and inferiority." But the vertical line exists in Gothic architecture as much more than a foil to vertical character; it checks and keeps it within bounds, and exhibits it as an expression of the infinite bounded and peacefully bounded by the finite—which is the true character of the life and worship symbolised. Hence the square-headed tower is as fine, if not a finer finish to the Gothic cathedral than the spire. Compare the tower of York with the spire of Freyburg in Breisgau—the finest spire in the world, rising as it does as a spire from the ground—and it will be found that the cessation of the great, steady heavenward current in York, gradually prepared for as it is by the treatment of the face of the tower, and culminating in the compromise of open battlements, each of which frames the pointed arch, creates a moresolemn and heart-expanding sense of infinite aspiration than the apparently greater flight of endeavour in the famous spire, which soars indeed twice the height of the tower, but, as it were, evaporates as it soars. The minds of the Gothic architects seem to have been much divided as to which was better: the checked and contained expression of the tower, in which an undiminished force of ascension was suggested, or the exhausting flight of the spire. The tower of Salisbury, for example, was not originally intended to carry the spire, which was added long after the cathedral was completed. They often obtained both features, giving a spire to only one of the west-end towers. There is, perhaps, no more satisfactory treatment of the west front than this, as may be seen in Strasburg Cathedral. Like many other fine effects, this most probably arose from accident—the accident of its not being convenient at the time to add the second spire; but that the incompleteness was fully recognised as a perfection is proved by the many instances of its having been, if not devised, allowed to remain.

There are three ways of treating the spire. It may commence at the earth, as that of Freyburg does, without the intervention of a tower; or it may rise from a tower the head of which is considerably larger than the base of the spire; orthe base of the spire may coincide with the top of the tower, in which case it is called a "broach spire." The second is the finest and by far the most frequent arrangement, as it combines the effects of spire and tower without confusing them; a part of the force of the tower being contained and checked, and a part being allowed to take its self-exhausting flight. It is to be observed, however, that even when the spire is most prominent—as in Lichfield, where there are three of them—it is, when compared with the whole building, only as it were an accidental escape and waste of the vast current of vertical force expressed by the entire mass of the building. Perhaps the most expressive treatment of the tower is in the innumerable examples in which only a very small proportion of its vertical force is permitted to escape in four or more pinnacles, one of which is often larger than the others. Spires and pinnacles are in most cases covered with lines of "crockets": figures in which ascending power is usually expressed by the upward growth of a leaf; which is emphasised by some check, made apparent to the eye by a strong bulge, like that of a current flowing over a stone. Wherever the idea of weight or side-thrust would occur naturally to the eye—as in buttresses, lower angles of gables, etc.—there is an especial outburst of flaming finial orpinnacle, or other mode of contradicting and reversing the idea, which the Greek architect would have been contented with accepting and beautifying.

Let us now enter the church, which is, within as well as without, a great geyser of ascending life; which may indeed lose itself in the dimness of the vaulted roof, as the spire loses itself in air, but never shows weariness of its flight or a memory of the earth from which it started. As in Egyptian and Greek architecture, so in the Gothic, we must look to the column for the strongest expression of the characterising idea. The Egyptian column suffered and seemed half-crushed under the weight it bore; the Greek rose to its burthen with the glad assurance of being fully adequate to its task. The Gothic is conscious of no task at all; but flies, without the least diminution of its substance, and without swelling either under sufferance or gathering of strength by entasis at any particular point, to the commencement of the arch; where it divides itself, sending up the streams of its clustered shafts, some into the lines of the arch and others to the top of the clerestory wall; then dividing again to follow the lines of the vaulting, there to meet like fingers joined in prayer, but still having no thought of the weight of the roof they really help to carry.

Mr. Ruskin complains of Gothic capitals—as he might also have done of Gothic bases—that they are unnecessary and ridiculous because they have no bearing power. If they had, they would cease to be Gothic, and the whole character of the wonderful art would be ruined. Capitals are sometimes entirely omitted, as in the shafted piers of Cologne; but when this is the case the point at which the arch springs becomes doubtful to the eye, and there is something exhausting in the wholly uninterrupted flight of the vertical lines. The capitals, like the horizontal *astragal* which often binds at intervals the clustered column, have no other purpose but to correct these effects of unrelieved continuity; and the mouldings of capitals, when they exist, not only have no and express no "bearing-power," but they very carefully express the contrary by various devices of undercutting, etc. It is the same with the base, when it is not altogether dispensed with. The most common form of Gothic base is a curious caricature of the Attic base, the form of which had been transmitted unimpaired to the Gothic architect through the Romanesque and Norman. It was perched upon and *overhung* a stilted plinth, which was itself a reversal of the expression of elementary support in the original flat plinth; and the curves of this base were so diminished in onepart and exaggerated in another that all reference to supporting power seemed to be derisively abolished. The "ogee" is a moulding which strongly expresses carrying power. A favourite Gothic base was two *reversed* ogees, the lower projecting far over the edge of the plinth, which, in classic architecture, always afforded a wide-spreading field for the base. And so on.

It would take a bulky volume to trace the wonderful integrity with which the three modes of envisaging the idea of weight are carried out in the three great architectures; but enough has been said to give the clue by which a fairly cultivated and perceptive student may follow up the subject for himself.

V

Before proceeding to consider the Norman and Moresque styles, a word should be said about that portion of Gothic decoration which does not directly help the main effect of aspiration—namely, cusped and foliated tracery, diaper-work, the foliage of spandrels, etc. etc. Kugler says: "This filling-in appears as a peculiar sort of architecture of independent signification." He does not, however, give the interpretation which he sees to be required. Yet there is an interpretation which only needs tobe put in words to be obvious to every eye which has made itself familiar with these objects. In exact proportion to the recognised perfection of these details, as it was attained in the middle or "decorated" period of pointed architecture, they become expressions of an idea almost identical with that which has been traced in the mode by which contented suspension or delay of the infinitely aspiring character in the main lines of the building is conveyed. As the inexhaustible torrent of upward life is checked peacefully, but with no denial of infinite *potential* aspiration, in the square-headed tower, so the same reconciliation of life with law without the least detriment to either—that reconciliation which is the consummation of Christianity—is expressed even more completely in the more essentially decorative details of pointed architecture. It is in the treatment of foliage that this character can be most easily traced, and this can be done best by comparing it with other modes of treatment. By the Greek architect this and other natural objects, when wanted for ornament, were what is called "conventionalised"; honeysuckles, roses, and waves of the sea were represented by certain formal figures which suited the lines of the architecture, and were not too much like nature to attract attention from those all-important lines to themselves. In the Italian Gothic, again, suchnatural objects are represented as nearly as possible like nature, but with such slight modifications and arrangements as were necessary to give them the consciousness of art. This is the sort of imitation which Mr. Ruskin recommends, and into which the northern Gothic fell in the decay of the art. But in fourteenth-century Gothic—that is to say, in the Gothic which was as much superior to that of the thirteenth and fifteenth centuries as the art of Athens was superior to that of Pæstum or Rome—nature was neither imitated nor conventionalised. The special aim of the fourteenth-century ornamentation is to show a vigorous life playing with perfect freedom in severely geometrical forms—with freedom so perfect that it is difficult to say whether the life shapes the law or the law the life. This highly and essentially symbolic character is the most marked expression of Gothic tracery. In its decay it took the form of licence and weakness in the French "flamboyant," and of hardness and rigidity in the English "perpendicular"; the life prevailing—to its own destruction—in the one, the lifeless law preponderating in the other. Gothic foliage, again, always *feels* the law; though, so far from suffering thereby, it is, in its place, far more beautiful than nature. The leafage not only follows geometrical outlines, but swells under its limitation into rich protuberances. The yearning for andpotentiality of infinite ascension, peacefully accepting its temporal limitations, and the freedom of life perfected by law, are the artistic motives of every detail as well as of the main masses of pure Gothic.

The Romano-Byzantine style attained in its final development, the "Norman," to the unity of idea which is the criterion of a true style. The arch up to this time had been treated partly as a thing of beauty in itself and partly as the constructive theme; in the Norman it took its place, expressionally, as subordinate to the wall, the mass of which it carries and distributes between the piers. The wall itself is the artistic theme of Norman architecture, and all decorative and some constructional features are devoted to making a boast of its *mass* and *thickness*. *Weight*—the theme in the three highly contrasted modes of the Egyptian, Greek, and Pointed architectures—plays no part in the Norman expression. The arch, being recognised by the eye for what it is, an infinitely powerful supporter, can express no proportion to finite superincumbent weight; and it is treated as a mere head to the gap in the wall between nave and aisle. The expressional intention of the Norman architects in this matter is curiously and decisively proved by the fact that their favourite arch-mouldings were the *billet* and *chevron*—i.e. lines of notches and angles which completely brokeup all idea of arch-character as referable to supporting power or to weight distributed on to the piers, and transferred the interest of the eye to the material substance of the wall out of which these figures were cut. The piers between these arches were huge masses of wall, either quadrangular or turned into great cylinders, without *entasis* or any other sign of having to bear anything; and such decoration as they had was devised so as to deny emphatically any reference to superimposed burthen. The figure of the weight-carrying shaft set in the angles of these piers was their principal decoration; but they were Lilliputian mockeries of the Attic shaft, or were twisted singly or doubly, and in various other ways ridiculed, as it were, the idea that shaft-*power* was demanded in the huge masses of masonry to which they were attached. The only thing that these little shafts—whether in notch of pier or in recess of porch, blind arcade, or window—ever carried or appeared to carry was a single line of the often innumerable mouldings, the purpose of which was simply to display the immense thickness of the wall, which was the true and only theme of this style. This system of emphasising the wall by negativing the shaft-power was occasionally carried into the almost grotesque excess of representing the shaft as broken in the middle! The favourite treatment of the Normanwall was to boast of its thickness exactly as the Doric shaft boasted of its supporting power—that is, by throwing away some portion of it. The face of the wall was recessed in panels, which were often filled with blind arcades. Modern builders often recess walls in this way in order to save material, leaving the wall thickest where it has most work to do; but the Norman and Lombard architects had no such economy in view. The windows and other apertures in the wall showed, by their shafted and moulded chamfers, the reality of thickness so great that the panelling and blank arcading was seen to *be* no sacrifice, though it was a delicate and effective suggestion of one. This arcaded panelling is not only on one plane of the wall-surface. The recessed plane is again recessed in the same way, and yet again, arcade within arcade; and finally, in the higher portions of the wall, open galleries are worked in its thickness. In apertures the constructive rule which requires that the bevel or chamfer should slant inwards, to give the better light, is sacrificed to the opportunity of showing the mass of the wall; and the chamfer is external, and is so treated in its decoration as to increase in every possible way the appearance of thickness. The treatment of the doorway, which is the point from which the expressional idea may be best enforced upon every beholder, is very peculiar. When there is no advanced porch, a deep arch is practised through a great part of the wall, and the thickness is emphasised by an elaborate perspective of shafts and mouldings. Within this deeply recessed arch the actual doorway is often worked as a horizontal-headed aperture in a plane face of wall without chamfer; the remaining thickness of the wall, not shown by the recessed arch, being thus left to be measured by the imagination, which has already been excited by the display of thickness within thickness of decorated archway. The Norman architects, in order still further to increase this effect, had sometimes recourse to a device that can scarcely be justified by strict architectural principles, which should never falsify construction in order to heighten expression. A face of wall was advanced in front of the main wall of the building, in order to obtain a much greater depth of masonry for showing off the multitudinously moulded entrance-arch. This projection did not form a real advanced porch, having its proper ecclesiastical purposes, but was nothing but a boast and display of mass in the masonry which really had no existence, the advanced face of wall concealing the fact that there was only mass enough behind it to allow of this misleading display. It may be said that the Gothic spire is constructed simply for display. It is quite true; but it is avowedly so constructed, and there was no concealment about it.

Mr. Ruskin, by the way, strangely affirms that "the direct symbolisation of a sentiment is a weak motive with all men"; inferring thence that there was no intention of aspiration in the Pointed architecture which he cares so little for. But surely the reverse is the case; and such symbolisation, in one way or other, constitutes a great part of the life of all men. The Gothic spire, which was the most costly as well as the most useless feature of the Gothic cathedral, is a final answer to such doctrine, which strikes indeed at the life of all artistic work. If it did not "symbolise a sentiment," what was done by it?

The round arch, which was the accident of the Norman architecture, being treated therein as a mere cavernous gap in masses of, in themselves, all-sufficient masonry, was, as it has been already said, adopted by the

Byzantine architects as the principal theme of their art; but this arch could be made nothing of, as the main source of expression, until it developed the dome; and the dome, as it proved, could not be made much of, until the Moresque builders took it in hand. It had the fatal defect, when on a large scale, of lateral thrust, which could only be met by a construction which had the double defect of positive and negativefalsehood. The domes of St. Sophia and St. Vitale, which the eye naturally presumes to be of one mass or substance with the substructure, are really formed, for lightness, of Rhodian bricks, pumice-stone, and coils of empty jars; and yet the lateral thrust is so great that it has to be opposed by a vast buttress-system, which is carefully concealed, because it would contradict, if exposed, the inevitable effect of extreme lightness in the dome. The Renaissance architects found themselves equally at a loss, as we know, in dealing with this feature. Both in St. Peter's and St. Paul's there is not one but two entirely separate domes. And when all is done the Byzantine and Renaissance domes are nothing to the eye but hollow shells, with no special artistic expression.

The Moresque architects hit upon the astonishing fancy of giving the dome *substance*, and thereby reconciling it with the constructive masses which supported and abutted upon it, and at the same time annihilating the idea of weight. This last idea already lurked in the Byzantine domes of St. Sophia, which seem to be carried wholly by "pendentives," and not at all by the piers to which these are attached. But it only lurked therein; for the eye necessarily inferred the immense lateral weight which piers and walls received. Now the honeycombed domes of the Moresque architectureare multiplied masses of pendentive forms hanging actually in air, and making it impossible for the eye to entertain any idea of lateral thrust in the whole or any part; and every detail of column, wall, and arch corroborates this fanciful negation of weight so perfectly that, for unity of effect, the Attic architecture remains the only rival of the Moresque, though there is this infinite difference between them: that, whereas the first appeals to the imagination and symbolises the Greek ideal of mental and moral equilibrium in forms of true construction, the latter only excites the fancy by a fairy tale. The whole carrying and resisting power of the arch is flung away by conferring upon it outlines which have no such power (the real carrying arch being hidden in the wall far outside the visible arch): the arches in colonnades, etc., seldom rest on, but simply abut against, the columns, which usually carry broad perpendicular beams, these being crossed above the arch-head by similar horizontal beams; so that there is only a small rectangular space of wall over each arch, and the idea of the weight of this being carried by the arch is contradicted by a network of bars carrying the lines of the wall into the upright beams. When a single arch is set in a wall, it is similarly framed in fretwork, the lines of which carry the eye off the arch without being pronounced enough to convey the idea that the force of the wall is thus conducted laterally to some support outside the arch.

It is impossible, in the space which can here be given to the matter, to notice one in a score of the details which combine to produce the effect with which every one is familiar. The purpose of these papers will have been answered if the vivifying thought of each of the five architectures which alone are integral styles, and not mixtures of styles, has been stated clearly, and such hints of the means by which such thought is conveyed have been given as will enable those who care to go further into the subject to do the rest of the analysis by themselves.

XXV

THOUGHTS ON KNOWLEDGE, OPINION, AND INEQUALITY

SOME learned men have maintained that we can know nothing. The truth is better stated by St. Paul: "If a man thinks that he knows anything, he knows nothing as he ought," that is nothing other than imperfectly. It is the more difficult to deal systematically with this matter, because we want, in our tongue, words of such relative meaning as *scire, cognoscere, intelligere,* etc. I propose only to run together a few such observations as simple good sense can make, and accept, and find use for.

A great and increasing proportion of persons would, if you asked them, maintain that all convictions are merely opinions. But it is not so. A fool may opine absolutely that a wise man is a fool, but the wise man knows that the fool is one. The same or opposite conclusions, political orotherwise, may be arrived at by two persons from a view of the same facts, and each may be equally confident; but the conclusions of one may be knowledge, and those of the other opinion. The reality of the difference is indicated by the difference of the feelings which commonly subsist between those who opine and those who know. Those who opine hate those who know, and who speak as those who know. They think it an assumption of superiority, whereas it is only its reality, and cannot but appear more or less in its manner of expression. Those who know, are only contemptuous or indifferent towards such as impudently or ignorantly opine. The consequence is that the knowledge which is wisdom is nowhere, as an acknowledged force and factor in worldly affairs, and is only able to assert itself *sub rosa*, or by accident, or by the more or less underhand management of folly and ignorance.

What most people call "deep and earnest convictions" on political and social topics are generally muddle-headed medleys of knowledge of fact and opinion. They know that such and such a thing is an evil, and they opine that they see a way to amend it; and if wiser people point out to them that the evil would not be so amended, or that greater evils would accrue from the attempt, they only feel that their "convictions" are affrontedand opposed by cold-blooded calculations. This kind of opinion is often as confident as actual knowledge. When Carlyle said that it was impossible to believe a lie, he can only have meant that it was impossible to believe it with that highest kind of certitude which consists in intellectual perception.

Probably no one could believe a lie with that degree of faith which would enable him to suffer deliberate martyrdom for it. Protestant and Catholic martyrs have usually been sufferers for one and the same faith, or, at least, parts of the same faith, in which parts they have considered the whole to be involved. Very few, if any, have ever carried the courage of mere "opinions" to the stake.

There can be no absolute certitude about the impressions of the senses or the inferences drawn from them. There can be about moral and spiritual things. The knave may sincerely opine that it is best for his interests to lie and cheat; but the honest man knows that he is a being whose interests are above all external contingencies, and that under certain circumstances it would be madness to behave otherwise than in a way which would be directly opposed to every argument and persuasion of the senses. It is only the mind of the most highly "scientific" constitution that will have its confidence in knowledge of this kind tried by considerations of its moral and intellectual obligations to Hottentots and Australian aborigines. "We can live in houses without being architects"; and we can know, without knowing or caring to know how we came by our knowledge. The house of the gods has lasted intact since Abraham and Hesiod, and shows no sign yet of tumbling about our ears.

The faculty of knowing, as differing from that of opining, seems, as might be expected from what has been said, to have as much to do with the character of the will as of the mind. To be honest, Shakespeare tells us, is to be one in ten thousand; and to discern intellectually, or to know, is a part, and a very great part, of honesty. A man may have learned a dozen languages, and have the whole circle of the sciences at his fingers' ends, and may know nothing worthy of being called knowledge; indeed, there is nothing which seems to be a greater hindrance to the acquisition of living knowledge than an engrossing devotion to the acquisition of words, facts, logical methods, and natural laws. It requires little learning to make a wise or truly knowing man, but much learning may not impossibly spoil one.

Mr. Matthew Arnold has said that a thorough classical education has often the same effects on a man's character as a grave experience. The reason is that it is a grave experience, a long series of small exercises of honesty, patience, and self-sacrifice, the sum of which is equal to a great and soul-sobering calamity. The author of the *Imitation* notes a kindred fact when he says, "No man can know anything till he is tried." Not only is the discipline of such an education, which, in its early stage at least has much in it that is repugnant and compulsory, fitted to qualify the character for the reception of true knowledge, but it conveys also, in an eminent degree, the matter of true knowledge. Without any disrespect to Mr. Huxley, Mr. Herbert Spencer, and Professor Max Müller, we may affirm that the man who knew Plato, Homer, and Æschylus rightly, and knew little else, would know far more than he who knew all that these great scientists could teach, and knew nothing else.

The man who knows, often finds himself at great disadvantage in the presence of fact-gatherers and persons who opine. His attitude is necessarily affirmative, and often, to the great scandal and contempt of his adversaries, simply affirmative. It does not enter into his calculations to have actively to defend a position which he sees to be impregnable; and when he leaves his proper occupation of "climbing trees in the Hesperides" to wield his club against those who know of no suchtrees, he is like a Hercules fighting mosquitoes. They cannot even see his club, and the conflict generally ends, as did that between the Lady and Comus, with an angry and wholly unconvincing assertion of incompetence.

Fain would I something say, yet to what end?
Thou hast nor ear, nor soul to apprehend
The sublime notion and high mystery
That must be utter'd to unfold the sage
And serious doctrine of virginity.
And thou art worthy that thou should'st not know
More happiness than is thy present lot.
Enjoy your dear wit and gay rhetoric,
That hath so well been taught her dazzling fence;
Thou art not fit to hear thyself convinced.

Wordsworth, in a still greater passion, calls his scientific adversary "a fingering slave." Of course this sort of thing tends to make the relations of the parties unpleasant; and in the eyes of the world the man of immense "information" and convinced ignorance goes off with the laurels.

Metaphysics for the most part is justly open to the objection that it attempts to explain things which Aristotle declares to be too simple to be intelligible—things which we cannot see with definiteness, not because they are beyond the focus of the mind's eye, but because they are too much within it. The metaphysician Hegel saysthat the sense of honour arises from our consciousness of infinite personal value. This may not be wholly satisfactory, but it is helpful; it is a part of the truth. But what do physicists make of such things as honour and chastity? They certainly endeavour to explain such ideas and feelings as they do everything else, but their explanations necessarily discredit these and all other things which profess to have "infinite value," and which wise men know to have infinite value.

The knowledge which can be made common to all, is a foundation upon which a certain increasing school, finding popular "opinion" too sandy, is endeavouring to build up a new state of things, religious, moral, political, and social. This kind of "positivism," which claims for its sanction the common, that is to say, the lowest experience of mankind, is and always has been the religion of the vulgar, to whatever class they belong. The growth of an unconscious and undogmatic positivism among the people at large is perhaps the most notable fact of the time. It shows itself not only in an increasing impatience of the notion that there is any reality which cannot be seen and felt, but in an intolerance even of any experience which is not, or cannot immediately be made, the experience of all. As boards and committees proverbially have to work on the level of the leastwise of their members, so the ideal perfection of this positivism would be government by the insight of the greatest dunderhead, since his experiences and perceptions alone would be sufficiently communicable to have the character of universality. Under such ideal conditions, every reality that makes life human would be completely eliminated. A man who should be detected in secretly entertaining principles of abstract honour, or trying to form his life upon the pattern of a beauty unknown to the arch-dunderhead, would fare as it fared in Athens with the man who dared to crown his house with a pediment; and vestries, consisting of the prophets of commonplace and popular experience, would vote everything in painting and poetry to be "bosh" which should be more esoteric in character than Frith's "Railway Station" or Martin Tupper's *Proverbial Philosophy*.

Science has already come very generally to mean, not that which may be known, but only such knowledge as every animal with faculties a little above those of an ant or a beaver can be induced to admit. Incommunicable knowledge, or knowledge which can be communicated at present only to a portion—perhaps a small portion—of mankind, is already affirmed to be no knowledge at all. A man who knows and acts up to his knowledge that it is better to suffer or inflictany extremity of temporal evil, rather than lie or cheat, though he may not be able to give any universally intelligible account of his knowledge, is already beginning to be looked upon as a prig or a fanatic; and chastity is already widely declared to be one of the "dead virtues," and marriage only legalised fornication, because "the sublime notion and high mystery that must be uttered to unfold the sage and serious doctrine" of purity must be taken, if taken at all by the many, upon trust.

The pure and simple ideal of life founded upon facts of universal experience is, however, too base ever to be perfectly attained in this world. There will always be a lingering suspicion with many that some have powers of discernment and an experience which are not granted to all; there will always be hidden heretics who will believe that there are realities which cannot be seen or touched by the natural eye or hand, or even by the rational perception of the many; and the present downward tendency may perhaps be checked, or at least delayed, by recalling to the minds of men that, as yet, we are all living more or less by faith in the better knowledge of the few, and by reminding them of that abyss towards which a new step is taken whenever any item of that knowledge is denied, in order towiden the foundations of the throne of popular experience.

The religion of universal experience must of course begin, as the dogmatic positivist insists, in the denial of God, or, what is exactly equivalent, in the assertion that, if God exists, He is altogether unknowable and removed from the practical interests of life. Now, let it be remembered that for a man to deny that God can be known is quite a different thing from his not being able to affirm, from positive knowledge, the reverse. A very small minority of mankind, but a minority which includes almost all who have attained the highest peaks of heroic virtue, and many who have been no less eminent for power of intellect and practical wisdom, have declared that, to them at least, God is knowable, communicable with, and personally discernible with a certainty which exceeds all other certainties; and they have further affirmed that this knowledge comes and can only come from a man's putting himself *en rapport* with the Divinity by an, in the beginning, more or less experimental faith, and by a conformity to the dictates of the highest conscience, so perfect as to involve, for a considerable period at least, laborious and painful self-denial. Now it would be placing oneself upon a level with such assertors of the highest knowledge to say that one knows that these declarationsare true, however strong the presumption of their truth may appear; but it is simply vulgar and brutal impudence for any one to assert positively that they are untruths or illusions, merely because his own experience and that of his pot-companions contains nothing which gives the least clue to their meaning. The *reductio ad absurdum* becomes complete when the same argument is carried into regions of more extended experience. A drunken bargeman has exactly the same right to deny the reality of the asserted experiences of a Petrarch or a Wordsworth as these would have to deny those of the saint or the apostle; and to descend a few steps farther, the amateur of abominable delights and the violator of natural relationships would justly, upon the widest experimental grounds, claim exemption from a condemnation chiefly founded upon an obscure perception and an intuitive horror of which he for his part had no experience.

Popular positivism will, however, always stop short of the length to which the doctrines of its prophets would lead it, and will, from time to time, be beaten back into the paths of the positivism of the nobler few on which all virtue and religion are founded, by finding itself in contact with the tremendous paradox, that the most universally beneficial and admired fruits of civilisation are and always have been gathered from trees of which the roots are wholly out of common view. The heroes themselves of the people will always refute popular experience better than any philosopher can. Though a Gladstone may dazzle them for a day by investing with a fatuous glamour the principles and platitudes with which the vulgar are familiar, it is to a Gordon, with inimitable courage and honour, the obvious outcome of unintelligible thoughts and experiences, that they will look with abiding reverence, and an elevating instinct that such men habitually move about in worlds by them unrealised.

The immense and unalterable inequalities in the knowing faculties of man are the source and in part the justification of that social inequality which roughly and very partially reflects them. Many otherwise amiable and conservative thinkers have, however, made the mistake of conceding that such inequality is, abstractedly considered, an evil, though a hopelessly incurable one. Conservative teaching would be much more effective than it is, were it more frequently occupied with proving that such inequality is no evil, but a very great good for all parties.

Dr. Johnson, who sometimes let fall, in off-hand talk, sayings of such depth, simplicity, and significance that we must go back to the philosophers of antiquity to find the like of them, once remarked that "inequality is the source of all delight." This saying, which must seem surprising to most modern ears, is absolutely true and even demonstrable.

All delight—not all pleasure, which is quite a different thing—will be found, when thoroughly examined, to consist in the rendering and receiving of love and the services of love. Hence the great and fortunately inextinguishable fountains of delight in the relationships of man and woman and of parents and children. It is true that a low and inorganic form of national polity may, to some extent, suppress even these pure springs of felicity; but, so long as there are women and children in the world, it can never become quite joyless. The doctrines of liberty, fraternity, and equality are known instinctively only by very bad children, and most women, when once they have been in love, repudiate such teaching indignantly, under whatever polity they may have been born.

Between unequals sweet is equal love;

and the fact is that there is no love, and therefore no sweetness, which is not thus conditioned; and the greater the inequality the greater the sweetness. Hence the doctrine that infinite felicity can only arise from the mutual love of beings infinitely unequal—that is, of the creator and the creature. Inequality, far from implying any dishonour on either side of the mutual compact of love, is the source of honour to both. Hooker, writing of marriage, says: "It is no small honour to a man that a creature so like himself should be subjected to him"; and we all know that the honour to woman which the chivalry of the middle ages made an abiding constituent of civilisation, was founded upon Catholic views of her subjection, and the obligation to give special honour, as of right, to the weaker vessel. Look also at the relations which usually subsist between an hereditary gentleman and his hereditary unequals and dependants, and compare them with the ordinary fraternal relations between a Radical master-tradesman and his workmen. The intercourse between the gentleman and his hind or labourer is free, cheerful, and exhilarating, because there is commonly in it the only equality worth regarding, that of goodwill; whereas the commands of the sugar-boiler or the screw-maker to their brothers are probably given with a frown and received with a scowl. Social inequality, since it arises from unalterable nature and inevitable chance, is irritating only when it is not recognised. The American plutocrat may be forced to travel for a week in the company of a hodman, becauseAmerican theories discountenance first and third class carriages; but catch him speaking to him! Whereas an English duke, if by chance thrown into the companionship of an honest countryman, would be on the best of terms with him before an hour was over, and the good understanding between the two would be made all the easier should the latter have on his distinguishing smock-frock. The genuine Tory is the most accessible of persons, the genuine Radical the least so. The one takes things as they are and must be, the other views them as they are not and cannot be, and, kicking against imaginary evils, often pays the penalty of finding himself firmly saddled with the realities.

"One can live in a house without being an architect," and it is not at all necessary that the common people should understand the English constitution in order to feel that their lives are the sweeter and nobler because they are members of its living organism. Not a ploughboy or a milkmaid but would feel, without in the least knowing why, that a light had passed from their lives with the disappearance of social inequalities, and the consequent loss of their dignity as integral parts of a somewhat that was greater than themselves.

The other day, walking in a country lane, I saw what appeared at a little distance to be a dyinganimal. On a closer view it proved to be the carcase of a sheep which had in great measure been actually transformed into a mass of the soft, white, malodorous grubs known to anglers by the name of gentles. The struggles of these creatures to get at the food which they concealed produced a strong and regular pulsation throughout the whole mass, and gave it a ghastly semblance of breathing. The ordered state of England, according to its ideal, which for many generations has been more or less realised, compared with the sort of democracy to which we are fast drifting and have wellnigh attained, is much like the animal in which myriads of individual organs, nerves, veins, tissues, and cells formed subordinated parts of one living thing, compared with this pulsating mass of grubs, each one of which had no thought but of its just share of carrion.

Democracy is only a continually shifting aristocracy of money, impudence, animal energy, and cunning, in which the best grub gets the best of the carrion; and the level to which it tends to bring all things is not a mountain tableland, as its promoters would have their victims think, but the unwholesome platitude of the fen and the morass, of which black envy would enjoy the malaria so long as all others shared in it. Whatever may be the pretences set forth by the leading advocates of such a state of things among us, it is manifest enough that black envy is the principal motive with many of them, who hate the beauty of the ordered life, to be ruling stars of which they cannot attain, just as certain others are said to "hate the happy light from which they fell." They hate hereditary honours, chiefly because they produce hereditary honour, and create a standard of truth and courage for which even the basest are the better in so far as they are shamed by it. Do the United States, some may ask, justify this condemnation? They are but a poor approach to the idea of democracy which seems now about to be realised among us: but they have already gone a long way towards extinguishing that last glory of, and now best substitute for, a generally extinct religion—a sense of honour among the people. "Why, what a dern'd fool you must be!" exclaimed a New York shopkeeper to a friend of mine, who had received a dollar too much in changing a note, and returned it. If there is a shopkeeper in England who would think such a thing, there is certainly not one who would dare to say it.

Nor, in losing sight of the sense of "infinite personal value," which is the source of honour and the growth of a long-enduring recognition of inevitable inequalities, have the Americans preserved delight. Dr. Johnson's saying finds a remarkable comment in the observation of a recent American traveller: "In the United States there is everywhere comfort, but no joy."

To conclude, it is quite possible to change the forms of social inequality, but to do away with the fact is of all things the most impossible. It is the trick or ignorance of the demagogue to charge existing inequalities with the evils and injustices in which they began, and with which they were attended for a long time afterwards. When conquest or revolution establishes the ever-inevitable political and social inequalities in new forms, it takes many generations of misery and turmoil to introduce into them the moral equality which renders them not only tolerable, but the source of true freedom and happiness.